MW01100229

Crash Course in Turbo C++

Namir Shammas

1985.

PROGRAMMING
SERIES

que

Crash Course in Turbo C++

Copyright© 1993 by Que® Corporation.

Library of Congress Catalog No.: 92-84090

ISBN: 1-56529-168-9

96 95 94 93   8 7 6 5 4 3 2 1

Interpretation of the printing code: the rightmost double-digit number is the year of the book's printing; the rightmost single-digit number, the number of the book's printing. For example, a printing code of 93-1 shows that the first printing of the book occurred in 1993.

Trademarks

Dedication

To my special childhood friend Bishara Freij

Credits

Publisher
Lloyd J. Short

Associate Publisher
Rick Ranucci

Publishing Manager
Joseph B. Wikert

Production Editors
Cheri Clark
Kezia Endsley

Technical Editor
Greg Guntle

Editorial Assistants
Elizabeth D. Brown
Stacey Beheler

Production Manager
Corinne Walls

**Proofreading/Indexing
Coordinator**
Joelynn Gifford

Production Analyst
Mary Beth Wakefield

Book Designer
Scott Cook

Cover Designer
Jay Corpus

Graphic Image Specialists
Dennis Sheehan
Jerry Ellis
Susan VandeWalle

Production
Jeff Baker
Julie Brown
Laurie Casey
Lisa Daugherty
Heather Kaufman
Bob LaRoche
Jay Lesandrini
Angela Pozdol
Linda Seifert
Sandra Shay
Phil Worthington

Indexer
Joy Dean Lee

Composed in *ITC Garamond* and *MCPdigital*
by Prentice Hall Computer Publishing

About the Author

Namir C. Shammas

Namir C. Shammas is a software engineer and an expert in object-oriented programming. He has authored and coauthored 30 books that deal with various programming languages.

Acknowledgments

I would like to thank many people at Que for working with me on this book. Many thanks to Joe Wikert, who contacted me to write the book and was actively involved in editing it. I thank the technical editor, Greg Guntle, for his valuable comments and corrections. My gratitude to editor Cheri Clark for ensuring the clarity of the text. Finally, many thanks to all the people at Que who were involved with the book.

Contents at a Glance

Table of Contents

10 Building Classes 127

11 Advanced Object-Oriented Programming 159

Introduction

This book teaches you to program with C++ in general, and with Turbo C++ Version 3.0 in particular. As part of the *Crash Course* book series, this book presents its topics at a fast pace, using relatively few and small examples.

This book takes a "no frills" approach to teaching the most important aspects of Turbo C++. It focuses on the key features of Turbo C++ so that the reader can begin writing practical applications quickly.

Who Should Use This Book?

This book is aimed at readers who want to learn the Turbo C++ programming language in the shortest amount of time possible. The audience includes nonprogrammers who can learn in a fast-track environment as well as programmers who are switching to Turbo C++.

What You Should Know To Use This Book

This book assumes that you are familiar with common computer terminology. Time is not wasted teaching you what an ASCII code is or how to write a batch file to start a C++ compiler. You should have a good grasp of basic computing principles before reading this book.

Organization of This Book

Crash Course in Turbo C++ is divided into 12 chapters.

Chapter 1 gives a brief background of C++ and a concise tour of the Turbo C++ integrated development environment (IDE).

Chapter 2 presents the first C++ program and explains the basic components of a C++ program. In addition, this chapter presents the compiler directives.

Chapter 3 talks about predefined data types, constants, variables, and operators.

Chapter 4 discusses the basic stream I/O and presents the functions that perform screen and cursor control.

Chapter 5 presents the decision-making constructs, which include the `if` and `switch` statements.

Chapter 6 talks about the various loops in C++. The loops include the versatile `for` loop as well as the conditional loops, `while` and `do-while`.

Chapter 7 discusses user-defined data types. These types include enumerated types, structures, and unions.

Chapter 8 presents reference variables, strings, and pointers. This chapter discusses pointers to simple types, strings, arrays, and structures.

Chapter 9 discusses C++ functions and covers a wide range of topics related to functions. Among these topics are function syntax, prototyping, function overloading, default arguments, and passing various kinds of parameters.

Chapter 10 looks at building a C++ class. This chapter discusses the various components of a class, including data members, member functions, friend functions, static members, and operators.

Chapter 11 presents more advanced topics related to class hierarchies. This chapter discusses class derivation, virtual functions, friend classes, and multiple inheritance.

Chapter 12 introduces the basics of file stream I/O using the C++ stream library. This chapter discusses sequential text I/O, sequential binary I/O, and random-access binary I/O.

Conventions Used

To get the most out of this book, you should know how it is designed. The following list introduces you to the general conventions used.

- New terms and emphasized words are presented in *italics*.

- Functions, commands, parameters, and the like are set in a special monospace text; for example, the main() function.

- User responses that must be typed at program prompts appear in **monospace bold**; for example:

  Enter a string: **No strings attached!**

- Placeholders (words that you replace with actual values) in code lines appear in *monospace italic*; for example:

  #define *constantName constantValue*

  In this example, you would replace *constantName* and *constantValue* with the appropriate name and number, depending, of course, on the program you were writing.

- Full programs appear as listings with numbered headings, whereas code fragments appear alone within the text.

- Throughout the book, you will see shaded boxes labeled "Syntax at a Glance." This design feature provides easy language reference to the essential elements of Turbo C++ programming. By providing this helpful information, *Crash Course in Turbo C++* will be not only a tutorial, but also a quick reference that will serve you for a long time to come. A sample Syntax-at-a-Glance box follows:

Syntax at a Glance

The *#include* Directive
The syntax of the #include directive is

```
#include <filename>
#include "filename"
```

The *filename* represents the name of the included file.

Examples:

```
#include <iostream.h>
#include "string.hpp"
```

■ In addition to Syntax-at-a-Glance boxes, you will find two
other visual pointers in this book:

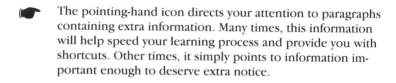

CAUTION

Caution boxes warn you of problem areas, including possible
cases in which you might introduce bugs into your program or
crash your system.

☞   The pointing-hand icon directs your attention to paragraphs
containing extra information. Many times, this information
will help speed your learning process and provide you with
shortcuts. Other times, it simply points to information important enough to deserve extra notice.

And Now...

Without any further delay, turn the page and begin learning to
master the Turbo C++ language.

The Turbo C++ IDE

This chapter discusses two main topics: the background of C++ and the integrated development environment (IDE) for Turbo C++ Version 3.x. In this chapter, you learn about the following topics:

- The history and basics of C++
- The Turbo C++ IDE
- The File option
- The Edit option
- The Search option
- The Run option
- The Compile option
- The Debug option
- The Project option
- The Options option
- The Windows option
- The Help option

C++ History and Basics

C++ was developed by Bjarne Stroustrup, at Bell Labs, the birthplace of C. Stroustrup developed C++ mainly as an object-oriented extension of C. Consequently, C++ shares much of its language syntax, keywords, and libraries with C. This approach enables C programmers to gradually move on to C++ without abandoning the C-based tools and utilities that they either developed or purchased.

The C++ language continues to evolve. Today, the evolution of C++ has moved from the hands of Bell labs to the ANSI C++ committee. This committee is working to standardize the C++ language and its main libraries.

Although C++ offers new object-oriented constructs to C programmers, there are some minor non-OOP differences between the two languages. These minor differences are found in the area of dynamic allocation (creating variables at runtime) and the declaration of user-defined types (records or structures that logically group data fields to make up a more coherent piece of information—a good example is a user-defined type that stores mailing addresses). Regarding the latter, C++ regards the tag names of user-defined types as type names. Another area of difference is I/O. Stroustrup introduced a new C++ mechanism that makes input and output more extendible than the C-style I/O, which is also available in C++. Although many C++ programmers use the STDIO.H for C-style I/O, many other C++ programmers recommend the sole use of the C++ stream I/O libraries.

The Turbo C++ IDE

Turbo C++ 3.x has an IDE that enables you to develop C++ applications very easily. The main component of the IDE, shown in Figure 1.1, is a text editor that highlights the C++ code using different colors for different program components.

The IDE displays windows that have the following components and features:

- Windows that can be moved and resized.
- A title bar that appears in the center of the top window frame. The window title is also the name of the edited file.
- A pair of vertical and horizontal scroll bars.
- A *zoom* box located at the upper-right edge of the window. This box enables you to zoom in on a window or restore it to its normal size.

■ A *close* box located at the upper-left edge of the window. This box enables you to quickly close a window.

■ A window number (available for the first nine windows) that appears to the left of the zoom box.

Close box

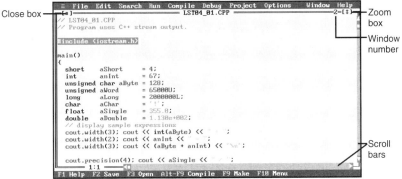

Zoom box

Window number

Scroll bars

Figure 1.1. *The general view of the Turbo C++ IDE.*

The IDE has a main menu, which contains the menu options shown in Table 1.1.

Table 1.1. The IDE main menu.

Menu Entry	Function
#	Repaints the desktop.
File	Manages files and directory operations, and exits the IDE.
Edit	Performs Clipboard operations and undoes the preceding changes. The Clipboard operations include Cut, Copy, and Paste.
Search	Searches for and replaces text, locates functions, and finds error locations in a file.
Run	Executes and traces a program.
Compile	Compiles, links, builds, and makes programs.
Debug	Manages the aspects of debugging a program. The selections in this option enable you to set and clear breakpoints and watch variables.

continues

Table 1.1. Continued	
Menu Entry	*Function*
Project	Manages project files that enable you to compile an application composed of multiple source code files.
Options	Views and alters the various default settings of Turbo C++. This menu has selections related to the compiler, the linker, colors, editors, directories, and the mouse.
Window	Manages displaying, closing, and arranging the various windows.
Help	Provides powerful online help.

The IDE menu options are discussed more fully in the following sections.

File

The File menu enables you to open and close files, print files, change directories, shell to DOS, and exit the IDE. You can use menu selections to open a window to edit either a new or an existing program. The File menu's selections enable you to save the contents of the currently selected window using either a new or the current filename. When you elect to save the currently edited text under a new filename, the IDE pops up a dialog box in which to enter the new filename. The IDE also offers an option for saving all the edited files in one swoop.

The IDE provides a menu selection for moving to another directory. A pop-up dialog box enables you to navigate to either the parent directory or the child subdirectories. Figure 1.2 shows the Change Directory dialog box.

Edit

The Edit menu has three sets of selections. The first set contains two items: Undo and Redo. These selections enable you to undo changes you made to your text and then redo them (or at least some of them). The second set of selections enables you to cut, copy, paste, and clear text, as well as copy examples from the Help system. The third selection set includes a single command that enables you to view the Clipboard.

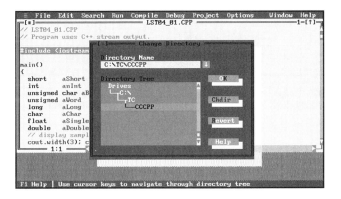

Figure 1.2. *The Change Directory dialog box.*

Search

The Search menu has selections that enable you to find and replace text. These selections use dialog boxes (see Figure 1.3, which shows the Replace Text dialog box) with several check boxes that enable you to fine-tune the operations. Using the check boxes, you can specify whether to search for whole words, use case-sensitive search, perform the search in the selected text block only, and so on.

Other selections in the Search menu enable you to move to a specific line number and move to the next or previous compilation errors.

Another menu selection is Locate Function, which displays the Locate Function dialog box. You type the name of a function to search for in this dialog box. This menu selection is available only during a debugging session.

Figure 1.3. *The Replace Text dialog box.*

Run

The Run menu contains selections that enable you to run a program normally or trace through it. The selections for debugging a program carry out the following actions:

- Executing the program at normal speed until you reach the statement where the cursor is located.

- Resetting the program.

- Going to the line where the cursor is currently placed.

- Tracing into statements. This mode of single-stepping enables you to trace function calls.

- Stepping over statements. This mode of single-stepping executes function calls at normal speed.

- Setting arguments.

The Run menu offers a selection that enables you to specify the command-line arguments from within the IDE.

Compile

The Compile menu has selections that enable you to perform the following tasks:

■ Compiling the currently selected file.

■ Updating the files listed in a project file that need recompilation—a valuable tool for multifile projects.

■ Recompiling all the files listed in a project file.

■ Linking the currently edited file.

■ Getting post-compilation information on the currently edited file. The information includes the size of the data and code of the compiled file.

■ Removing the messages from the Messages window.

Debug

The Debug menu enables you to monitor the program execution and observe the program's data.

The Inspect option opens an Inspector window, where you can inspect values in a data element. The data type of the element you inspect defines the type of information presented in the window. Turbo C++ enables you to inspect simple data types, arrays, pointers, structures, unions, functions, and classes.

The Evaluate/Modify option enables you to perform the following tasks:

■ Evaluate a variable or an expression.

■ View the value of any variable or other data item.

■ Modify the value of simple data items.

The Call Stack option pops up the Call Stack dialog box to show the sequence of functions your program called to reach the function that's currently executing.

The Watches option opens the Watches submenu, which contains commands that control the use of watchpoints. You can add, edit, or delete a watch, or remove all watches. Figure 1.4 shows the Watch window.

The Toggle Breakpoint option enables you to set or clear an unconditional breakpoint on the line where the cursor is positioned. The IDE highlights a breakpoint that you set.

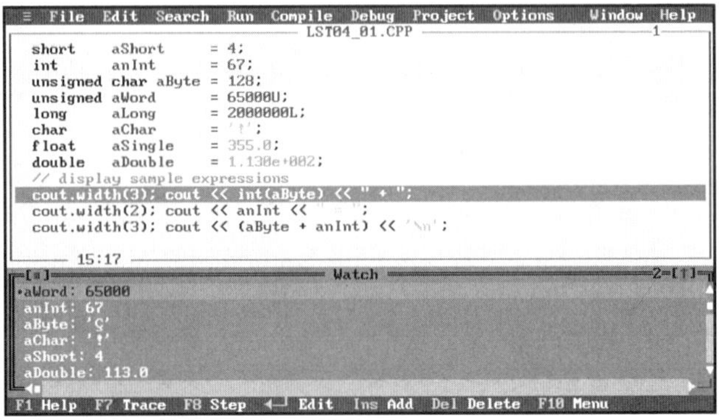

Figure 1.4. *The Watch window.*

Project

Projects are special files that enable you to compile and link a multifile application. Using the selections in the Project menu, you can open a new or an existing project file, add or remove source-code files to it, recall include files, and view project file options.

Options

The Options menu contains many selections and subselections. The following items appear on this menu:

- Application: Enables you to elect to compile your file as a standard application, as an overlay, or as a library.

- Compiler: Offers a nested menu that enables you to fine-tune the operations of the Turbo C++ compiler. Among the items you can set are the memory mode, the use of compiled headers, and the generation of debug information. This item includes the following subselections:

  - Source: Tells the compiler to expect certain types of source code.

  - Messages: Sets choices that affect error message reporting for that category of errors. Among these categories are ANSI violations, C++ warnings, frequent errors, and portability.

■ Names: Displays the Segment Names dialog box, which enables you to change the default segment, group, and class names for code, data, and BSS sections.

■ Transfer: Displays the Transfer dialog box, where you can add or remove programs to or from the ≡ menu (the System menu). You select items from the ≡ menu to run another program without actually leaving Turbo C++.

■ Make: Displays the Make dialog box, where you set conditions for project management.

■ Linker: Displays other menus and dialog boxes that enable you to fine-tune the operations of the linker.

■ Librarian: Manages creating files used in the linking process.

■ Debugger: Displays the Debugger dialog box, where you choose options that affect the integrated debugger.

■ Directories: Specifies include, lib, and output directories.

■ Environment: Opens a menu of commands that you use to customize Turbo C++ with environment-wide settings. These settings influence the preference, the editor, the mouse, the desktop, the colors, and the startup.

■ Save: Offers options to save the edited file, the project file, and the desktop.

Windows

The Windows menu has selections that enable you to manage various windows. Using these selections, you can resize and move windows, zoom in and out on a window, tile or cascade the various windows on the desktop, select the next window, close the currently selected window, close all the windows, and list all the windows. The Window menu also enables you to open the Message, Output, Watch, User Screen, Register, Project, and Project Notes windows.

Help

The Help menu provides access to the online Help system. The online Help comes up in a special Help window. The text in the

Help window is a help screen. The selections of the Help options enable you to get help by looking at the various topics, selecting an item by index, searching for a topic, and moving back to the preceding topic. You can also get help on using the Help system itself.

The Help system offers information on virtually all aspects of the IDE and Turbo C++. In addition, the system displays one-line menu and dialog-box hints on the status line whenever you choose a menu selection or a dialog-box item. Figure 1.5 shows a sample Help window.

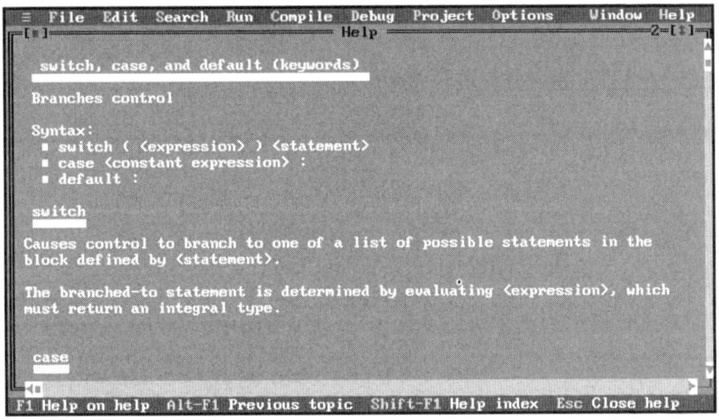

Figure 1.5. *A sample Help window.*

Summary

This chapter gave you a brief history of C++ and discussed the menu options and selections of the Turbo C++ IDE. The chapter offered the following information:

- C++ extends the C language mainly in the area of object-oriented programming.

- The File menu manages files and directory operations, and exits the IDE.

- The Edit menu performs Clipboard operations and undoes the preceding edit changes. The Clipboard operations include Cut, Copy, and Paste.

- The Search menu searches for and replaces text, locates functions, and indicates error locations in a file.

- The Run menu executes and traces a program.

- The Compile menu compiles, links, builds, and makes programs.

- The Debug menu manages the aspects of debugging a program. The selections in this menu enable you to set and clear breakpoints and watch variables.

- The Project menu manages project files that enable you to compile an application made up of multiple source code files.

- The Options menu views and alters the various default settings of Turbo C++. Among the options are those related to the compiler, the linker, colors, editors, directories, and the mouse.

- The Windows menu manages displaying, closing, and arranging the various windows.

- The Help menu provides powerful online help.

Getting Started

Your journey in the world of C++ begins in this chapter, which presents the following basic topics:

■ Getting started with C++

■ The various compiler directives

A Simple C++ Program

If you have ever programmed in another language, the first C++ program that I present will probably take you down memory lane. The simple program displays a one-line greeting message. This program enables you to see the very basic components of a C++ program.

Listing 2.1 contains the source code for the LST02_01.CPP program, which displays the words "Hello, Programmer!"

Listing 2.1. The source code for the LST02_01.CPP program.

```
// LST02_01.CPP
// A trivial C++ program that says hello

#include <iostream.h>

main()
{
  cout << "Hello, Programmer!";
  return 0;
}
```

Examine this code. Notice the following characteristics of a C++ program:

- The comments in C++ use the // characters for comments that run to the end of the line. C++ also supports the C-style comments that begin with the /* characters and end with the /*characters.

- The C++ program supports two levels of code: global and functions (C++ functions cannot contain nested functions). In addition, the function main() plays an important role, because program execution begins with this function. Therefore, a C++ program can have only a single main() function. You can place the main() function anywhere in the code. Because main() is a function, just like any other C++ function, it can have its own local data types, constants, and variables. In addition, the main() function should return a value, just like any other function.

- C++ strings are enclosed in double quotation marks, and characters are enclosed in single quotation marks. Thus, 'A' is a character, whereas "A" is a single-character string. Therefore, C++ handles 'A' and "A" differently.

- C++ defines blocks using the { and } characters.

- Every statement in a C++ program ends with a semicolon.

- This C++ program contains an #include compiler directive that instructs the Turbo C++ compiler to include the IOSTREAM.H header file. Header files offer a central resource for definitions and declarations used by your program. The IOSTREAM.H provides the operations that support basic stream input and output.

- The C++ program outputs the string "Hello, Programmer!" to the standard output stream, cout, which is usually the screen. In addition, the program uses the extractor operator, <<, to send the emitted string to the output stream.

- The main() function must return a value that reflects the error status of the C++ program. Returning the value 0 signals to the operating system that the program terminated normally.

Compiler Directives

C++ supports various compiler directives, including #define, #undef, #include, #error, #if (and other related directives), #line, and #pragma. The next sections cover these directives.

The *#define* Directive

The preprocessor examines your C++ source code to locate the #define macro directive. The #define directive is a tool for defining constants and pseudofunctions.

The *#define* Directive

The syntax of the #define directive is

```
#define macro macro_text_or_value
#define macro(parameter_list) macro_expression
```

The *macro_text_or_value* represents the text or value that replaces the macro. The *parameter_list* is a list of parameters that can give a macro great flexibility in generating different results.

Examples:

```
#define GRAVITY 9.81
#define ABS(x) ((x) < 0) ? (-x) : (x)
```

The first form of the #define directive defines a macro-based constant. The second form reveals that you can include parameters with the macro. This feature makes macros very flexible. C++ requires that a line cannot contain more than one #define directive. If you cannot contain the macro expression in one line, you can use the \ character (with a leading space) as a line-continuation code. Macros that possess parameters enable you to create pseudofunctions. Compared with formal functions, these macro-based functions are faster but require more code space. The additional code space is necessary because the preprocessor substitutes every occurrence of these macros with their respective expressions.

The #define directive serves the following purposes:

■ Defines constants.

■ Replaces reserved words or symbols with others.

■ Creates pseudo data type identifiers using standard data types.

■ Creates shorthand commands.

■ Defines macro-based pseudofunctions.

The *#undef* Directive

The counterpart of the #define directive is #undef. This directive undefines a macro. The #undef macro enables you to erase the names of unneeded macros to recuperate the space they occupy and reduce the possibility of conflict with other data items that have the same names.

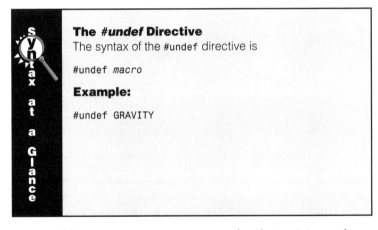

The *#undef* Directive
The syntax of the #undef directive is

#undef *macro*

Example:

#undef GRAVITY

C++ enables you to reuse a macro name by placing it in another #define directive. You need not use the #undef directive to explicitly clear a macro definition between two #define directives.

The *#include* Directive

The #include directive enables you to include the source lines from another file into the current one, as though you typed the included file.

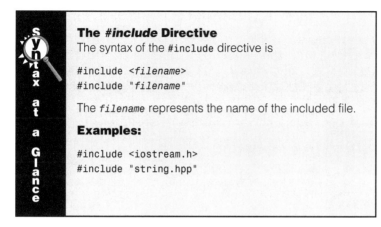

The #*include* Directive
The syntax of the #include directive is

```
#include <filename>
#include "filename"
```

The *filename* represents the name of the included file.

Examples:

```
#include <iostream.h>
#include "string.hpp"
```

The two forms differ in how the #include directive searches for the included file. The first form searches for the file in the special directory for included files as specified in the IDE Directories menu selection in the Options menu option. The second form expands the search to include the current directory.

The #*error* Directive

The #error directive generates an error message. It is useful, for example, to signal errors such as incompatible versions.

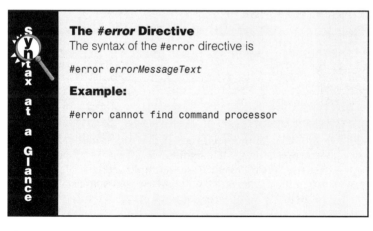

The #*error* Directive
The syntax of the #error directive is

```
#error errorMessageText
```

Example:

```
#error cannot find command processor
```

The preceding directive may yield an error message that looks like the following message:

```
Error: filename line 19 : Error directive : cannot find
command processor
```

The Conditional Compilation Directives

The #if directive enables you to perform conditional compilation of your C++ program. Turbo C++ provides the #if, #elif, #else, and #endif directives to support conditional compilation.

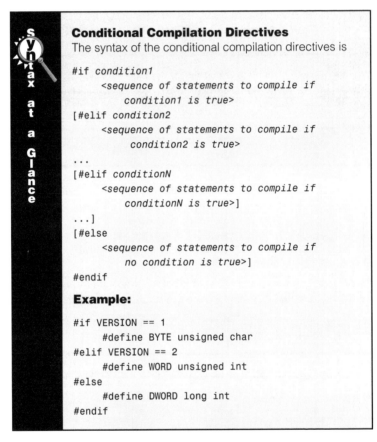

Conditional Compilation Directives
The syntax of the conditional compilation directives is

```
#if condition1
     <sequence of statements to compile if
         condition1 is true>
[#elif condition2
     <sequence of statements to compile if
         condition2 is true>
...
[#elif conditionN
     <sequence of statements to compile if
         conditionN is true>]
...]
[#else
     <sequence of statements to compile if
         no condition is true>]
#endif
```

Example:

```
#if VERSION == 1
     #define BYTE unsigned char
#elif VERSION == 2
     #define WORD unsigned int
#else
     #define DWORD long int
#endif
```

The conditional compilation directives are very useful in compiling specific statements only when conditions are either true or false. These directives enable you to have multiple versions of a program that reside in the same source file. You can generate each version of a program by defining certain macros that are associated with each version.

The *#ifdef* and *#ifndef* Directives

C++ provides additional conditional compilation directives. The #ifdef directive compiles a set of lines if a macro *is* defined. The #ifndef directive compiles a set of lines if a macro *is not* defined.

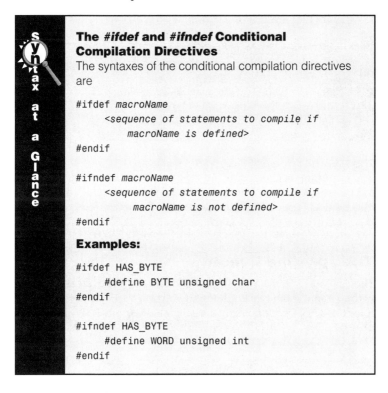

Syntax at a Glance

The *#ifdef* and *#ifndef* Conditional Compilation Directives

The syntaxes of the conditional compilation directives are

```
#ifdef macroName
    <sequence of statements to compile if
        macroName is defined>
#endif

#ifndef macroName
    <sequence of statements to compile if
        macroName is not defined>
#endif
```

Examples:

```
#ifdef HAS_BYTE
    #define BYTE unsigned char
#endif

#ifndef HAS_BYTE
    #define WORD unsigned int
#endif
```

The *#line* Directive

The #line directive enables you to specify the line number to a program for cross-referencing or reporting an error either in the preprocessor or for compilation purposes. This directive is especially useful in working with a large number of modules.

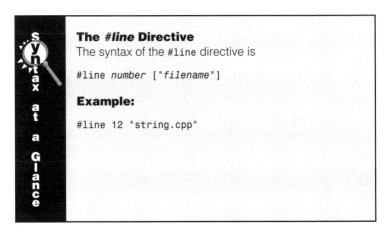

The #line directive enables you to specify the location of the line number in the original file rather than the location of the line in the preprocessed file. The latter may vary if you include other files—a likely event. The `filename` clause is needed only the first time you use the #line directive.

The *#pragma* Directive

The #pragma directive supports implementation-specific directives without affecting other implementations of C++. If a C++ compiler does not support a specific pragma directive, it simply ignores it.

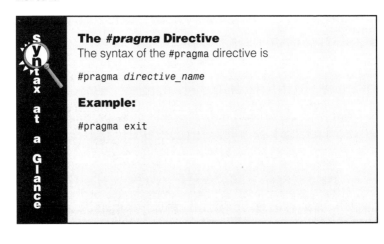

The Turbo C++ Version 3.x compiler has the following #pragma directives:

■ The #pragma startup statement instructs the compiler to execute a specific function *before* the main() function when you start a program. The syntax of this directive is

```
#pragma startup function [priority]
```

The optional *priority* parameter is an integer in the range of 64 to 255. When it is omitted, the compiler assigns the default value of 100. The lower values have a higher priority. Using the priorities with the #pragma startup, you can specify multiple startup functions and the order of executing them before calling function main().

■ The #pragma exit directive specifies the function that is called *after* the main() function when you end a program. The syntax of this directive is

```
#pragma exit function [priority]
```

The *priority* parameter (similar to the one used in #pragma startup) specifies the order of executing the functions after function main().

■ The #pragma hdrfile directive specifies the name of the file that stores the precompiled headers. Precompiled headers speed up recompiling a program, because the header files are compiled once and need not be recompiled. The default name for the file that stores the precompiled headers is TCDEF.SYM. The syntax of this directive is

```
#pragma hdrfile "filename.SYM"
```

■ The #pragma hdrstop directive ends the list of files that are eligible for precompilation.

■ The #pragma inline directive tells the compiler that there are inline assembly language statements in the source code.

■ The #pragma option directive enables you to specify command-line options in your source code. The syntax of this directive is

```
#pragma option [options...]
```

For example, the directive

```
#pragma option -Dversion=1.0
```

defines the identifier version and assigns it the string 1.0.

■ The #pragma saveregs directive ensures that a huge function will not alter the values of any of the CPU registers when it is called. Such functions normally use additional CPU registers to handle the address segment and offset. Consequently, you may lose valuable information in the additional CPU registers. The #pragma saveregs directive protects you from such loss.

■ The #pragma warn directive enables you to check the Display Warning settings (in the Options | Compiler | Messages dialog box) or override the -wxxx warning command-line option. The syntax of the #pragma warn is

```
#pragma warn [+ ¦ - ¦ .]xxx
```

The + symbol turns on the warn pragma. The - symbol turns off the warn pragma. The dot symbol restores the warn pragma to the value it had when the file compilation started.

■ The #pragma argused directive is strictly permitted between function definitions and affects only the next function. This directive disables the warning message which indicates that a certain parameter is never used in a function. The syntax of this #pragmadirective is

```
#pragma argused
```

Summary

In this chapter, you started your journey of learning C++. You learned about the following topics:

■ The basic components of a C++ program. These include comments, the main() function, and the declaration of simple variables.

■ Turbo C++'s support of the following directives:

　　■ The #define directive, which is used to define macros.

　　■ The #undef directive, which enables you to undefine a macro.

■ The #include directive, which enables you to include files to be compiled with the currently compiled source file.

■ The #error directive, which generates an error message.

■ The conditional compilation directives, which enable you to perform conditional compilation of your C++ program.

■ The #line directive, which enables you to specify the line number to a program for cross-referencing or reporting an error.

■ The #pragma directive, which supports implementation-specific directives.

C H A P T E R
T H R E E

Variables and Operators

Data types, constants, variables, and operators are vital components of a language that you employ to write terms, factors, and expressions. This chapter presents the following topics:

- Predefined data types

- Constants

- Variables

- Arithmetic operators

- Increment and decrement operators

- Arithmetic assignment operators

- The sizeof operator

- Typecasting and data conversion

- Relational and logical operators

- Bit-manipulation operators

- The comma operator

Predefined Data Types

C++ offers the int, char, float, double, and void data types. The void data type is a special valueless type. C++ adds more flexibility to data types by supporting what are known as *data type modifiers.* These modifiers alter the precision and the range of values. The type modifiers are signed, unsigned, short, and long.

Constants

C++ offers constants in two flavors: macro-based and formal. The macro-based constants are inherited from C and use the #define compiler directive (which is covered in Chapter 2, "Getting Started"). The second type of constant in C++ is the formal constant.

The Formal Constant
The syntax of the formal constant is

```
const dataType constantName = constantValue;
```

The *dataType* item is an optional item that specifies the data type of the constant values. If you omit the data type, the C++ compiler assumes the int type.

Examples:

```
const unsigned daysInWeek = 7;
const hoursPerDay = 24;
```

CAUTION

Many C++ programmers, including the gurus behind C++ itself, have spoken against using the #define directive to define constants. They favor the formal constants, because these enable the compiler to perform type checking.

Variables

Variables and other identifiers in C++ are case sensitive. The name of a variable must begin with a letter and can contain other letters, digits, and the underscore character. The names of variables in Turbo C++ are significant to any length. When you declare a variable in a program, you must associate a data type with it. C++ enables you to assign a value to variables when you declare them.

Declaring Variables
The syntaxes for declaring variables are

```
type variableName;
type variableName = initialValue;
```

Examples:

```
int i;
double x = 3.14;
```

C++ enables you to declare a list of variables that have the same types in a declaration statement. For example:

```
int j, i = 2, k = 3;
double x = 3.12;
double y = 2 * x, z = 4.5, a = 45.7;
```

The initializing values can include other previously defined variables or constants.

Arithmetic Operators

Table 3.1 shows the C++ operators. The compiler performs floating-point or integer division, depending on the operands. If both operands are integer expressions, the compiler produces the code for an integer division. If either operand or both operands are floating-point expressions, the compiler yields code for floating-point division.

Table 3.1. The C++ arithmetic operators.

Operator	Purpose	Data Type	Example
+	Unary plus	Numeric	`x = +y + 3;`
-	Unary minus	Numeric	`x = -y;`
+	Add	Numeric	`z = y + x;`

continues

Table 3.1. Continued

Operator	Purpose	Data Type	Example
-	Subtract	Numeric	z = y - x;
*	Multiply	Numeric	z = y * x;
/	Divide	Numeric	z = y / x;
%	Modulus	Integer	z = y % x;

The Increment and Decrement Operators

C++ provides special increment and decrement operators, ++ and
--. These operators enable you to increment and decrement by
one the value stored in a variable.

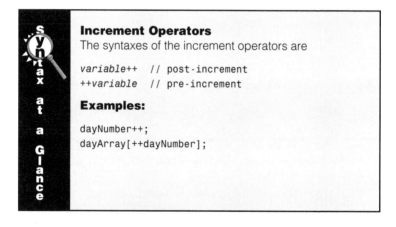

Increment Operators
The syntaxes of the increment operators are

```
variable++   // post-increment
++variable   // pre-increment
```

Examples:

```
dayNumber++;
dayArray[++dayNumber];
```

This syntax indicates that there are two ways to apply the ++ and --
operators. Placing these operators to the left of their operands alters the value of the operand *before* the operand contributes its
value in an expression. Similarly, placing these operators to the
right of their operands changes the value of the operand *after* the
operand contributes its value in an expression. If the ++ or -- operators are the only operators in a statement, there is no difference
between using the pre- and post- forms.

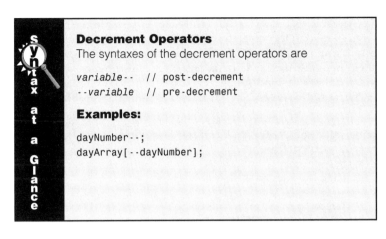

Here are a few simple examples:

```
int i, j, k = 5;
k++; // k is now 6, same effect as ++k
--k; // k is now 5, same effect as k--
k = 5;
i = 4 * k++; // k is now 6 and i is 20
k = 5;
j = 4 * ++k; // k is now 6 and j is 24
```

The first statement uses the post-increment ++ operator to increment the value of variable k. If you wrote ++k instead, you would get the same result when the statement finished executing. The second statement uses the pre-decrement -- operator. Again, if you wrote k-- instead, you would get the same result. The next two statements assign 5 to variable k and then use the post-increment ++ operator in a simple math expression. This statement multiplies 4 by the current value of k (that is, 5), assigns the result of 20 to the variable i, and then increments the values in variable k to 6. The last two statements show a different outcome. The last statement first increments the value in variable k (the value in variable k becomes 6), performs the multiplication, and then assigns the result of 24 to the variable j.

The Assignment Operators

As a programmer, you often come across statements like these:

```
IndexOfFirstElement = IndexOfFirstElement + 4;
GraphicsScaleRatio = GraphicsScaleRatio * 3;
CurrentRateOfReturn = CurrentRateOfReturn / 4;
DOSfileListSize = DOSfileListSize - 10;
IndexOfLastElement = IndexOfLastElement % 23;
```

The variable that receives the result of an expression is also the first operand. (Of course, the addition and multiplication are communicative operations. Therefore, the assigned variable can be either operand with these operations.) Notice that I chose relatively long names to remind you, perhaps, of the need to shorten the expression without making the names of the variables shorter.

C++ offers assignment operators that combine simple math operators and the assignment operator. For example, you can write the following statements:

```
IndexOfFirstElement += 4;
GraphicsScaleRatio *= 3;
CurrentRateOfReturn /= 4;
DOSfileListSize -= 10;
IndexOfLastElement %= 23;
```

Notice that the name of the variable appears only once. Also notice that the statements use the operators +=, *=, /=, -=, and %=. Table 3.2 shows these arithmetic assignment operators. C++ supports other types of assignment operators as well (see Table 3.5).

Table 3.2. The arithmetic assignment operators.

Operator	Long Form	Short Form
+=	x = x + y;	x += 12;
-=	x = x - y;	x -= y;
*=	x = x * y;	x *= y;
/=	x = x / y;	x /= y;
%=	x = x % y;	x %= y;

The *sizeof* Operator

Often your programs need to know the byte size of a data type or variable. C++ provides the `sizeof` operator, which takes for an argument either a data type or the name of a variable (`scalar`, `array`, `record`, and so on).

The *sizeof* Operator
The syntax of the sizeof operator is

sizeof(*variable_name* ¦ *data_type*)

Example:

sizeDiff = sizeof(long) - sizeof(int);

Typecasting

Automatic data conversion is one of the duties of a compiler. This data conversion simplifies expressions and relieves the frustration of both novice and veteran programmers. With behind-the-scenes data conversion, you need not study each expression that mixes somewhat similar data types in your program. For example, the compiler handles most expressions that mix various types of integers or that mix integers and floating-point types. You get a compile-time error if you try to do something illegal!

Typecasting
C++ supports the following forms of typecasting:

type_cast(*expression*)

and

(*type_cast*) *expression*

Example:

```
int x = 2;
double y, z;
y = double(x);
z = (double) x;
```

The two statements convert the int type of variable x into a double number stored in variables y and z. Each statement shows you a different way to write a typecast.

Relational and Logical Operators

The relational and logical operators are the basic building blocks of decision-making constructs in any programming language. Table 3.3 shows the C++ relational and logical operators. Notice that C++ does not spell out the operators AND, OR, and NOT. Instead, it uses single- and dual-character symbols. Also notice that C++ does not support the relational XOR (exclusive OR) operator. You can use the following #define macro directives to define the AND, OR, and NOT identifiers as macros if you prefer to use descriptive symbols rather than the cryptic single- and dual-character symbols:

```
#define AND &&
#define OR ||
#define NOT !
```

Although these macros are permissible in C++, you will most likely get a negative reaction from veteran C++ programmers who read your code.

Table 3.3. The C++ relational and logical operators.

Operator	Meaning	Example
&&	Logical AND	a && b
||	Logical OR	c || d
!	Logical NOT	!c
<	Less than	i < 0
<=	Less than or equal to	i <= 0
>	Greater than	j > 10
>=	Greater than or equal to	x >= 8.2
==	Equal to	c == '\0'
!=	Not equal to	c != '\n'
?:	Conditional assignment	k = (i<1) ? 1 : i;

The operators in Table 3.3 are typically used by decision-making constructs (Chapter 5 discusses the if and switch statements) and by loops (Chapter 6 discusses the for, do-while, and while loops).

CAUTION

I want to warn you here about erroneously using the = operator as the equality relational operator. This common mistake is a source of logical bugs in a C++ program. You might have been accustomed to using the = operator in other languages for testing the equality of two data items. In C++, you must use the == operator. So what happens if you employ the = operator in C++? Do you get a compiler error? You might get a compiler warning. Other than that, your C++ program should run. Of course, a session with such a program will probably lead to bizarre program behavior, or even a system hang! When the program reaches the expression that is supposed to test for equality, it actually attempts to assign the operand on the right of the = sign to the operand on the left of the = sign. Here is an example:

```
int i = 10;
int j = 20;
int areEqual;
areEqual = (i = j);
```

The last statement assigns the value of variable j to variable i and then to variable areEqual. As the name of the areEqual variable suggests, the intent of the code writer is to assign the result of the relational expression that compares the contents of variables i and j. The correct statement is

```
areEqual = (i == j);
```

Looking at Table 3.3, you might have noticed the last operator, ?:. This special operator supports what is known as the *conditional expression*. The conditional expression is shorthand for a dual-alternative simple if-else statement (more about the if statement in Chapter 5, "Decision Making"):

```
if (condition)
     variable = expression1;
else
     variable = expression2;
```

The equivalent conditional expression is

```
variable = (condition) ? expression1 : expression2;
```

The conditional expression tests the condition. If that condition is true, it assigns *expression1* to the target variable. Otherwise, it assigns *expression2* to the target variable.

Bit-Manipulation Operators

The C++ programming language is suitable for system development. System development requires bit-manipulation operators to toggle, set, query, and shift the bits of a byte or word. Table 3.4 shows the bit-manipulation operators. Notice that C++ uses the symbols & and ¦ to represent the bitwise AND and OR, respectively. Recall that the && and ¦¦ characters represent the *logical* AND and OR operators, respectively. In addition to the bit-manipulation operators, C++ supports the bit-manipulation assignment operators, shown in Table 3.5.

Table 3.4. The bit-manipulation operators in C++.

Operator	Meaning	Example
&	Bitwise AND	i & 128
¦	Bitwise OR	j ¦ 64
^	Bitwise XOR	j ^ 12
~	Bitwise NOT	~j
<<	Bitwise shift left	i << 2
>>	Bitwise shift right	j >> 3

Table 3.5. The C++ bit-manipulation assignment operators.

Operator	Long Form	Short Form
&=	x = x & y;	x &= y;
¦=	x = x ¦ y;	x ¦= y;
^=	x = x ^ y;	x ^= y;
<<=	x = x << y;	x <<= y;
>>=	x = x >> y;	x >>= y;

The Comma Operator

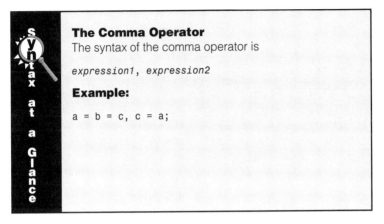

The Comma Operator

The syntax of the comma operator is

```
expression1, expression2
```

Example:

```
a = b = c, c = a;
```

The comma operator requires the program to completely evaluate the first expression before evaluating the second expression. Notice that both expressions are *located in the same C++ statement.* What does "located in the same C++ statement" mean, exactly? Why utilize this rather unusual operator in the first place? These questions have a lot of merit. The comma operator with its peculiar role does serve a specific and very important purpose in the for loop (which you will learn about in Chapter 6). As you will see in Chapter 6, using the comma operator enables you to create multiple expressions that initialize multiple loop-related variables.

Now that you have read about most of the C++ operators (Chapter 8 discusses a few more operators that deal with pointers and addresses), there are two related aspects you need to know. First, the *precedence* of the C++ operators. Second, the *direction* (or sequence) of evaluation. Table 3.6 shows the C++ precedence of the C++ operators covered so far and also indicates the evaluation direction. The precedence values quantify the precedence of the various operators—especially for some operators that are in the same category but have a different precedence. These values are not actually used by the compiler.

Table 3.6. The C++ operators and their precedence.

Name	Symbol	Evaluation Direction	Precedence
Unary			
Post-increment	++	Left to right	2
Post-decrement	- -	Left to right	2
Address	&	Right to left	2
Bitwise NOT	~	Right to left	2
Typecast	(*type*)	Right to left	2
Logical NOT	!	Right to left	2
Negation	-	Right to left	2
Plus sign	+	Right to left	2
Pre-increment	++	Right to left	2
Pre-decrement	- -	Right to left	2
Size of data	sizeof	Right to left	2
Multiplicative			
Modulus	%	Left to right	3
Multiply	*	Left to right	3
Divide	/	Left to right	3
Additive			
Add	+	Left to right	4
Subtract	-	Left to right	4
Bitwise Shift			
Shift left	<<	Left to right	5
Shift right	>>	Left to right	5
Relational			
Less than	<	Left to right	6
Less or equal	<=	Left to right	6
Greater than	>	Left to right	6
Greater or equal	>=	Left to right	6
Equal to	==	Left to right	7
Not equal to	!=	Left to right	7

Name	Symbol	Evaluation Direction	Precedence
		Bitwise	
AND	&	Left to right	8
XOR	^	Left to right	9
OR	¦	Left to right	10
		Logical	
AND	&&	Left to right	11
OR	¦¦	Left to right	12
		Ternary	
Cond. express.	?:	Right to left	13
		Assignment	
Arithmetic	=	Right to left	14
	+=	Right to left	14
	-=	Right to left	14
	*=	Right to left	14
	/=	Right to left	14
	%=	Right to left	14
Shift	>>=	Right to left	14
	<<=	Right to left	14
Bitwise	&=	Right to left	14
	¦=	Right to left	14
	^=	Right to left	14
Comma	,	Left to right	15

Summary

This chapter presented the following topics:

- The predefined data types.

- The two flavors of constants in C++. These include the macro-based constants and the formal constants.

- Variables in C++, which must be associated with data types and can be initialized during their declaration.

■ The arithmetic operators, including the +, -, *, /, and % (modulus).

■ The increment and decrement operators. These operators come in the pre- and post- forms. C++ enables you to apply these operators to variables that store characters, integers, and even floating-point numbers.

■ The arithmetic assignment operators, which enable you to write shorter arithmetic expressions in which the primary operand is also the variable receiving the result of the expression.

■ The sizeof operator, which returns the byte size of either a data type or a variable.

■ Typecasting, which enables you to force the type conversion of an expression.

■ Relational and logical operators that enable you to build logical expressions. C++ does not support a predefined Boolean type and instead considers 0 as false and any nonzero value as true.

■ The conditional expression, which offers a short form for the simple dual-alternative if-else statement (to be covered in Chapter 5).

■ The bit-manipulation operators that perform bitwise AND, OR, XOR, and NOT operations. In addition, C++ supports the << and >> bitwise shift operators.

■ The bit-manipulation assignment operators that offer short forms for simple bit-manipulation statements.

■ The comma operator, which is a very special operator. It separates multiple expressions in the same statements and requires the program to completely evaluate one expression before evaluating the next one.

C H A P T E R

FOUR

Managing I/O

C++ does not define I/O operations that are part of the core language. Instead, C++ relies—like its parent language, C— on I/O libraries to provide the needed I/O support. This chapter looks at the basic input and output operations and functions that are supported by the IOSTREAM.H and CONIO.H header files. In this chapter, you learn about the following topics:

- Formatted stream output

- Stream input

- Character I/O functions

- Screen control

- Cursor control

Formatted Stream Output

Listing 4.1 shows how to use the standard output stream to create formatted output. The IOSTREAM.H contains functions that specify the width and the number of digits for floating-point numbers.

Listing 4.1. The source code for the LST04_01.CPP program.

```
// LST04_01.CPP
// Program uses C++ stream output

#include <iostream.h>

main()
{
  short    aShort    = 4;
  int      anInt     = 67;
  unsigned char aByte = 128;
  unsigned aWord     = 65000U;
  long     aLong     = 2000000L;
  char     aChar     = '!';
  float    aSingle   = 355.0;
  double   aDouble    = 1.130e+002;
  // display sample expressions
  cout.width(5); cout << aWord << " - ";
  cout.width(2); cout << aShort << " = ";
  cout.width(5); cout << (aWord - aShort) << '\n';

  cout.width(3); cout << int(aByte) << " + ";
  cout.width(2); cout << anInt << " = ";
  cout.width(3); cout << (aByte + anInt) << '\n';

  cout.width(7); cout << aLong << " / ";
  cout.width(5); cout << aWord << " = ";
  cout.width(3); cout << (aLong / aWord) << '\n';

  cout.precision(4); cout << aSingle << " / ";
  cout.precision(4); cout << aDouble << " = ";
  cout.precision(5); cout << (aSingle / aDouble) << '\n';

  cout << "The character saved in variable aChar is "
       << aChar << '\n';
  return 0;
}
```

Consider the statements that perform the stream output. The program in Listing 4.1 uses the stream function width() to specify the output width for the next item displayed by a cout << statement. Notice how many statements are needed to display three integers. In addition, notice that the program uses the expression int(aByte) to typecast the unsigned char type into an int. Without this type conversion, the contents of variable aByte appear as a character. If you use the stream output to display integers that have default widths, you can indeed replace the six stream output statements with a single statement.

The last set of stream output statements outputs the floating-point numbers. Here the program uses the stream function `precision()` to specify the total number of digits to display. Again, it takes six C++ statements to output three floating-point numbers. Again, if you use the stream output to display numbers that have default widths, you can replace the six stream output statements with a single statement.

Stream Input

Like the standard output stream, C++ offers the standard input stream, `cin`. This input stream is able to read predefined data types, such as `int`, `unsigned`, `long`, and `char`. Typically, you use the inserter operator `>>` to get input for the predefined data types.

Listing 4.2 shows the source code for the program LST04_02.CPP. The program simply multiplies two numbers. The program prompts you to enter the numbers to multiply. You must delimit these two items with a space and must end your input by pressing the Enter key. The program gets your input using the following statement:

```
cin >> x >> y;
```

This statement gets the values for the variables x and y from the standard input stream, `cin`. The input operation uses the inserter operator `>>`.

Listing 4.2. The source code for the LST04_02.CPP program.

```
// LST04_02.CPP
// Program illustrates standard stream input

#include <iostream.h>

main()
{
  double x, y, z;

  cout << "Enter two numbers: ";
  cin >> x >> y;
  z = x * y;
  cout << x << " * " << y << " = " << z << "\n";
  return 0;
}
```

Character I/O Functions

Turbo C++ offers other functions to support character I/O. Some of these functions are prototyped in the header file CONIO.H and might not be portable to other C++ implementations. The following character input functions are available:

■ The getche() function, which returns a character from the console and echoes that character on-screen. This function is prototyped in the header file CONIO.H.

■ The getch() function, which returns a character from the console but does not echo that input character. This function is also prototyped in the header file CONIO.H.

■ The getchar() function, which returns a character from the console. This function is prototyped in the header file STDIO.H.

The following character output functions are available:

■ The putch() function, which emits a single character to the console. This function is prototyped in the header file CONIO.H.

■ The putchar() function, which emits a single character to the console. This function is also prototyped in the header file STDIO.H.

The getchar() and putchar() functions work with input and output devices in general and not just the console. Examples of other input and output devices are communications ports and the printer.

☞ The character input functions need no argument and return an int type that represents the ASCII code of the input character. Why not return a char type? The answer points back to the traditional approach of C, inherited by C++. The traditional approach draws a very close association between integers and characters (which are always stored using their numeric ASCII code). Therefore, each character input function merely returns a character in its *raw* form—an ASCII code integer. The same logic is applied to the character output functions, which accept an int type rather than a char type.

It's time to put some of the character I/O functions to work. The following simple program prompts you to enter three characters.

The program uses the getche() and getch() functions to enter each character. Notice that the call to getch() is followed by a call to putch() to echo the input character on the console. The functions getche() and getch() do not require you to press Enter. Consequently, these functions support fast character input. On the other hand, these functions give you no chance to correct your erroneous input! The program uses the putch() function to emit the three characters you type. Listing 4.3 contains the source code for program LST04_03.CPP.

Listing 4.3. The source code for the LST04_03.CPP program.

```
// LST04_03.CPP
// Program demonstrates character I/O using getche, getch,
// and putch

#include <iostream.h>
#include <conio.h>

main()
{
    char char1, char2, char3;

    cout << "Type the first character: ";
    char1 = getche();
    cout << "\nEnter a second character: ";
    char2 = getch(); putch(char2);
    cout << "\nEnter a third character : ";
    char3 = getch(); putch(char3);
    cout << "\n\nYou entered ";
    putch(char1);
    putch(char2);
    putch(char3);
    cout << "\n\n";
    getch();
    return 0;
}
```

Here is a sample session with the program in Listing 4.3:

```
Type the first character: a
Enter a second character: b
Enter a third character : c

You entered abc
```

Screen Control

The CONIO.H header file declares two functions that enable you to clear the screen and clear to the end of a line:

■ The function clrscr(), which clears the screen and places the cursor at the top-left corner of the screen. The declaration of function clrscr() is

```
void clrscr(void);
```

■ The function clreol(), which clears to the end of the current line. The declaration of function clreol() is

```
void clreol(void);
```

Cursor Control

The CONIO.H header file declares three functions that enable you to set and query the location of the cursor on-screen:

■ The function gotoxy(), which moves the location of the cursor to a specified location. The declaration of the function gotoxy() is

```
void gotoxy(int x, int y);
```

The parameters x and y specify the screen row and column numbers, respectively.

■ The functions wherex() and wherey(), which return the row and column number of the cursor location, respectively. The declarations of these two functions are

```
int wherey(void);
int wherex(void);
```

Consider a program that manipulates the cursor using the gotoxy(), wherex(), and wherey() functions. Listing 4.4 shows the source code for the program LST04_04.CPP. The program displays the letter *o* as it moves from the upper-left corner of the screen in the lower-right direction for a few lines.

Listing 4.4. The source code for the LST04_04.CPP program.

```
// LST04_04.CPP
// Program illustrates cursor control

#include <conio.h>
#include <dos.h>

main()
{
  clrscr();
  gotoxy(wherex() + 1, wherey() + 1);
  putch('o');
  delay(200);
  gotoxy(wherex() - 1, wherey());
  putch(' ');
  gotoxy(wherex() + 1, wherey() + 1);
  putch('o');
  delay(200);
  gotoxy(wherex() - 1, wherey());
  putch(' ');
  gotoxy(wherex() + 1, wherey() + 1);
  putch('o');
  delay(200);
  gotoxy(wherex() - 1, wherey());
  putch(' ');

  return 0;
}
```

Summary

This chapter examined the basic input and output operations and functions that are supported by the IOSTREAM.H, STDIO.H, and CONIO.H header files. You learned about the following topics:

■ Formatted stream output, which uses the precision and width to provide some basic formatting output.

■ Standard stream input, which supports the insert operator >> to get input for the predefined data types in C++.

■ Character I/O functions, which rely on the I/O libraries. Among these libraries is the CONIO.H file, which defines the character input function `getche()` and `getch()`, as well as the character output function `putch()`.

■ Screen control, which employs the `clrscr()` and `clreol()` functions (declared in file CONIO.H) to clear the screen and to clear to the end of the line.

■ Cursor control, which can be handled by the functions `gotoxy()`, `wherex()`, and `wherey()` (declared in file CONIO.H) to set and query the cursor location.

Decision Making

In any programming language, the decision-making constructs enable applications to examine conditions and specify courses of action. The different programming languages vary in the features of their decision-making constructs. This chapter looks at the decision-making constructs in C++ and covers the following topics:

■ The single-alternative `if` statement

■ The dual-alternative `if-else` statement

■ The multiple-alternative `if-else` statement

■ The multiple-alternative `switch` statement

The Single-Alternative *if* Statement

So far, the programs you have seen executed every statement, no exceptions. Now, you will learn how to alter program flow using the `if` statement. C++ offers various forms of the `if` statement enabling you to select single-, dual-, and multiple-alternative courses of action.

C++ uses the open and close braces to define a block of statements. Listing 5.1 shows a program with a single-alternative `if` statement. The program prompts you to enter a positive number and stores the input in the variable x. If the value in x is greater than or equal to zero, the program displays the square root of x.

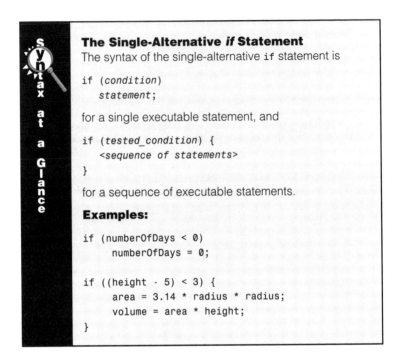

The Single-Alternative *if* Statement

The syntax of the single-alternative `if` statement is

```
if (condition)
    statement;
```

for a single executable statement, and

```
if (tested_condition) {
    <sequence of statements>
}
```

for a sequence of executable statements.

Examples:

```
if (numberOfDays < 0)
    numberOfDays = 0;

if ((height - 5) < 3) {
    area = 3.14 * radius * radius;
    volume = area * height;
}
```

Listing 5.1. The source code for the LST05_01.CPP program.

```cpp
// LST05_01.CPP
// Program demonstrates the single-alternative if statement

#include <iostream.h>
#include <conio.h>
#include <math.h>

main()
{
  double x;
  clrscr();
  cout << "Enter a positive number: ";
  cin >> x;
  if (x >= 0)
    cout << "The square root of " << x
         << " is " << sqrt(x) << "\n";
  getch();
  return 0;
}
```

Here is a sample session with the program in Listing 5.1:

```
Enter a positive number: 25
The square root of 25 is 5
```

The Dual-Alternative *if-else* Statement

This form of the if statement offers two routes of action based on the tested condition. The else keyword separates the statements used to execute each alternative.

The Dual-Alternative *if-else* Statement
The syntax of the if-else statement is

```
if (condition)
    statement1;
else
    statement2;
```

for a single executable statement in each clause, and

```
if (tested_condition) {
    <sequence #1 of statements>
}
else {
    <sequence #2 of statements>
}
```

for a sequence of executable statements in both clauses.

Example:

```
if (quantity > 9) {
    discount = 0.1;
    price = qnty * itemPrice * (1 - discount);
}
else {
    discount = 0;
    price = qnty * itemPrice;
}
```

Consider an example that uses the dual-alternative `if` statement. Listing 5.2 contains the source code for the program LST05_02.CPP. This program prompts you to enter a character and stores your input in the variable c. The program converts your input into uppercase, using the function `toupper()` (declared in the CTYPE.H header file) and then uses a dual-alternative `if` statement to determine whether you entered a vowel. The statement in each alternative displays a message confirming whether you entered a vowel.

Listing 5.2. The source code for the LST05_02.CPP program.

```
// LST05_02.CPP
// Program demonstrates the dual-alternative if statement

#include <iostream.h>
#include <conio.h>
#include <ctype.h>

main()
{
  char c;
  clrscr();
  cout << "Enter a character: ";
  cin >> c;
  c = toupper(c);
  if (c == 'A' || c == 'I' || c == 'O' ||
      c == 'E' || c == 'U')
    cout << "You entered a vowel letter\n";
  else
    cout << "You entered a nonvowel letter\n";
  getch();
  return 0;
}
```

Here is a sample session with the program in Listing 5.2:

```
Enter a character: g
You entered a nonvowel letter
```

Potential Problem with the *if* Statements

There is a potential problem with the dual-alternative `if` statement. This problem occurs when the `if` clause contains another single-alternative `if` statement. In this case, the compiler thinks that the `else` clause belongs to the nested `if` statement. Here is an example:

```
if (i > 0)
    if (i = 10)
        cout << "You guessed the magic number";
else
    cout << "Number is out of range";
```

In this code fragment, when `i` is a positive number other than 10, the code displays the message `Number is out of range`. The compiler treats the preceding statements as though the code fragment meant

```
if (i > 0)
    if (i = 10)
        cout << "You guessed the magic number";
    else
        cout << "Number is out of range";
```

To correct this problem, enclose the nested `if` statement in a statement block:

```
if (i > 0) {
    if (i = 10)
        cout << "You guessed the magic number";
}
else
    cout << "Number is out of range";
```

These examples illustrate how the compiler matches the `else` with the closest `if`, unless you use braces to clarify the intent of the `if` statements.

The Multiple-Alternative *if-else* Statement

C++ enables you to nest `if-else` statements to create a multiple-alternative form. This alternative provides your applications a lot of power and flexibility.

The multiple-alternative `if-else` statement performs a series of cascaded tests until one of the following situations occurs:

■ One of the conditions in the `if` clause or in the `else if` clauses is true. In this case, the accompanying statements are executed.

■ None of the tested conditions is true. The program executes the statements in the catchall else clause (if there is an else clause).

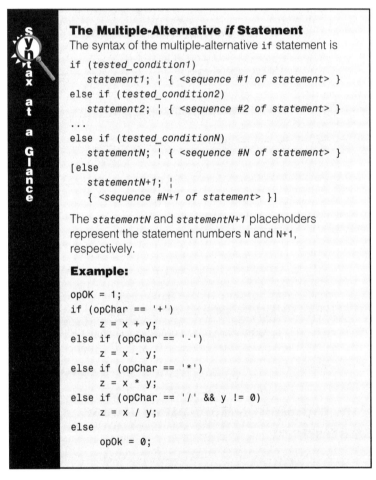

The Multiple-Alternative *if* Statement
The syntax of the multiple-alternative if statement is

```
if (tested_condition1)
    statement1; ¦ { <sequence #1 of statement> }
else if (tested_condition2)
    statement2; ¦ { <sequence #2 of statement> }
...
else if (tested_conditionN)
    statementN; ¦ { <sequence #N of statement> }
[else
    statementN+1; ¦
    { <sequence #N+1 of statement> }]
```

The *statementN* and *statementN+1* placeholders represent the statement numbers N and N+1, respectively.

Example:

```
opOK = 1;
if (opChar == '+')
    z = x + y;
else if (opChar == '-')
    z = x - y;
else if (opChar == '*')
    z = x * y;
else if (opChar == '/' && y != 0)
    z = x / y;
else
    opOk = 0;
```

Listing 5.3 shows a program that uses the multiple-alternative if statement to determine which of the following characters an entered character is

■ An uppercase letter.

■ A lowercase letter.

■ A digit.

■ A non-alphanumeric character.

The program uses an if clause to determine whether the variable c stores an uppercase letter. The program uses two else if clauses to determine whether the variable c contains a lowercase letter or a digit. The catchall else clause detects that variable c does not store an alphanumeric character.

Listing 5.3. The source code for the LST05_03.CPP program.

```
// LST05_03.CPP
// Program demonstrates the multiple-alternative if statement

#include <iostream.h>
#include <conio.h>
#include <ctype.h>

main()
{
  char c;
  clrscr();
  cout << "Enter a character: ";
  cin >> c;
  if (c >= 'A' && c <= 'Z')
    cout << "You entered an uppercase letter\n";
  else if (c >= 'a' && c <= 'z')
    cout << "You entered a lowercase letter\n";
  else if (c >= '0' && c <= '9')
    cout << "You entered a digit\n";
  else
    cout << "You entered a non-alphanumeric character\n";
  getch();
  return 0;
}
```

Here's sample output from this program:

```
Enter a character: !
You entered a non-alphanumeric character
```

The Multiple-Alternative *switch* Statement

The switch statement offers a special form of multiple-alternative decision making. It enables you to examine the various values of an integer-compatible expression and select the appropriate outcome.

The *switch* Statement

The syntax of the `switch` statement is

```
switch (expression) {
    case constant1_1:
[   case constant1_2: ...]
        <one or more statements>
        break;
    case constant2_1:
[   case constant2_2: ...]
        <one or more statements>
        break;
...
    case constantN_1:
[   case constantN_2: ...]
        <one or more statements>
        break;
    default:
        <one or more statements>
}
```

The general case labels are identified by specifying the alternative number, followed by the underscore and the value number. For example, `constant2_1` stands for the first value in the second alternative of the `switch` statement.

Example:

```
opOK = 1;
switch (opChar) {
    case '+':
        z = x + y;
        break;
    case '-':
        z = x - y;
        break;
    case '*':
        z = x * y;
        break;
```

```
        case '/':
            if (y != 0)
                z = x / y;
            else
                opOK = 0;
            break;
        default:
                opOk = 0;
}
```

The following rules apply to using the switch statement:

■ The switch requires an integer-compatible value. This value can be a constant, a variable, a function call (discussed in more detail in Chapter 9), or an expression. The switch statement does not work with floating-point data types.

■ The value after each case label *must* be a constant.

■ C++ does not support case labels with ranges of values. Instead, each value must appear in a separate case label.

☞■ You need to use a break statement after each set of executable statements. The break statement causes program execution to resume after the end of the current switch statement. If you do not use the break statement, the program execution resumes at the subsequent case labels.

■ The default clause is a catchall clause.

■ The set of statements in each case label or grouped case label need not be enclosed in open and close braces.

☞ The lack of single case labels with ranges of values makes using a multiple-alternative if-else statement more appealing if you have a large contiguous range of values.

Listing 5.4 shows a modified version of Listing 5.3. The new program performs the same task of classifying your character input, this time using a switch statement. If you examine the listing, you will notice that I included only a few case labels to keep the program listing short. This program also provides a case when using the if-else statements is actually more suitable than using the switch statement.

Listing 5.4. The source code for the LST05_04.CPP program.

```
// LST05_04.CPP
// Program demonstrates the multiple-alternative
// switch statement

#include <iostream.h>
#include <conio.h>
#include <ctype.h>

main()
{
  char c;
  clrscr();
  cout << "Enter a character: ";
  cin >> c;
  switch (c) {
    case 'A':
    case 'B':
    case 'C':
    // other case labels
      cout << "You entered an uppercase letter\n";
      break;
    case 'a':
    case 'b':
    case 'c':
    // other case labels
      cout << "You entered a lowercase letter\n";
      break;
    case '0':
    case '1':
    case '2':
    // other case labels
      cout << "You entered a digit\n";
      break;
    default:
      cout << "You entered a non-alphanumeric character\n";
  }
  getch();
  return 0;
}
```

Here is a sample session with the program in Listing 5.4:

```
Enter a character: 2
You entered a digit
```

Summary

This chapter presented the various decision-making constructs in C++. These constructs include:

- The single-, dual-, and multiple-alternative `if` statements. The `if` statements require you to observe the following rules:

    - You must enclose the tested condition in parentheses.

    - You must enclose blocks of statements in pairs of open and close braces.

- The multiple-alternative `switch` statement, which offers a more readable alternative to lengthy `if/else if` blocks.

Loops

Loops are powerful language constructs that enable computers to excel in performing repetitive tasks. This chapter presents the following loops and loop-related topics in C++:

- The `for` loop statement

- Arrays

- Using `for` loops to create open loops

- Skipping loop iterations

- Exiting loops

- The `do-while` loop statement

- The `while` loop statement

The *for* Loop

The `for` loop in C++ is a versatile loop because it supports
fixed as well as conditional iteration. The latter feature of the
`for` loop does not have a parallel in many popular programming languages, such as Pascal and BASIC.

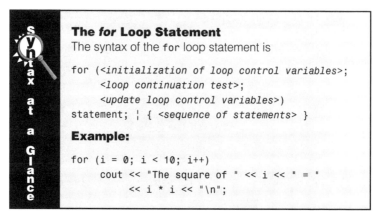

The *for* Loop Statement

The syntax of the for loop statement is

```
for (<initialization of loop control variables>;
     <loop continuation test>;
     <update loop control variables>)
statement; ¦ { <sequence of statements> }
```

Example:

```
for (i = 0; i < 10; i++)
    cout << "The square of " << i << " = "
         << i * i << "\n";
```

The for loop statement has three components, all optional. The first component initializes the loop control variables. I use the plural of *variable* here to indicate that C++ enables you to employ more than one loop control variable. The second part of the loop is the condition that determines whether the loop makes another iteration. The last part of the for loop is the clause that increments or decrements the loop control variables.

☞ The C++ for loop enables you to declare the loop control variables. Such variables exist in the scope of the loop. The inner for loop in Listing 6.1 shows this feature.

Consider an example that shows the fixed loop. The example in Listing 6.1 prompts you to enter an integer in the range of 1 to 50 and calculates the factorial number for that integer. The program uses a fixed loop to get the factorial. If you enter a number outside the range of 1 to 50, the program displays an error message.

Listing 6.1. The source code for the LST06_01.CPP program.

```
// LST06_01.CPP
// Program calculates a factorial using a for loop

#include <iostream.h>
#include <conio.h>

main()
{
    // factorial is declared and also initialized
    double factorial = 1.0;
```

```
    int n;

    clrscr();
    cout << "Enter the factorial of [1..30]: ";
    cin >> n;
    if (n > 0 && n <= 30) {
        for (int i = 1; i <= n; i++)
            factorial *= (double) i;
        cout << n << "! = " << factorial << "\n";
    }
    else
        cout << "Sorry! factorial is out of range\n";
    getch();
    return 0;
}
```

Listing 6.1 uses the following loop to calculate the factorial:

```
for (int i = 1; i <= n; i++)
    factorial *= (double) i;
```

Notice that the loop declares the loop control variable i. The loop uses this variable to update the value stored in the variable factorial. The loop initializes the loop control variable by assigning it a value of 1. The loop continuation test is the expression i <= n. The loop increment clause is i++, which increments the loop control variable by 1. You can also write the loop in Listing 6.1 in two other ways:

```
for (int i = 1; i <= n; i += 1)
    factorial *= (double) i;
```

or

```
for (int i = 1; i <= n; i = i + 1)
    factorial *= (double) i;
```

The loop increment in Listing 6.1 is the best form and the one typically used by C++ programmers.

You can modify the program in Listing 6.1 to use a downward-counting for loop. Here is how the loop would look:

```
for (int i = n; i > 0; i--)
    factorial *= (double) i;
```

To use increments other than one, you can rewrite the for loop in Listing 6.1 like this:

```
for (int i = 1; i <= n; i += 2)
    factorial *= (double) i * (i + 1);
if ((n/2)*2) != n) factorial /= n+1;
```

This `for` loop iterates about half as many times as the one in Listing 6.1. Each iteration multiplies the variable factorial by the expression `i * (i + 1)`. The `if` statement after the loop adjusts the result for odd values of variable n.

The next program, shown in Listing 6.2, modifies Listing 6.1 so that the `for` loop only uses the loop continuation test. What about the other two components of the `for` loop? The loop control variable, `i`, is declared with the other local variables in the `main()` function. The variable `i` is also initialized with the value of 1. Therefore, the `for` loop need neither declare nor initialize the loop control variable. As for the loop increment, the post-increment operator is used in the statement that updates the factorial value. This approach absolves the loop itself from incrementing the control variable.

Listing 6.2. The source code for the LST06_02.CPP program.

```
// LST06_02.CPP
// Program calculates a factorial using a for loop

#include <iostream.h>
#include <conio.h>

main()
{
    // factorial is declared and also initialized
    double factorial = 1.0;
    int n, i = 1;

    clrscr();
    cout << "Enter the factorial of [1..30]: ";
    cin >> n;
    if (n > 0 && n <= 30) {
        for (; i <= n;)
            factorial *= (double) i++;
        cout << n << "! = " << factorial << "\n";
    }
    else
        cout << "Sorry! factorial is out of range\n";
    getch();
    return 0;
}
```

Arrays

C++ supports arrays that vary in dimensions. The typical number of array dimensions used in most applications decreases as the number of dimensions increases. Most applications use single-dimensional arrays. Some programs use two-dimensional arrays, and a few specialized applications employ three-dimensional arrays, or higher.

Single-Dimensional Arrays

C++ supports single-dimensional and multi-dimensional arrays. You can declare arrays for the predefined data types as well as for user-defined types.

Single-Dimensional Arrays
The syntax for declaring a single-dimensional array is

```
type arrayName[numberOfElements];
```

Examples:

```
char aString[45];
double monthlyIncome[12];
```

C++ supports arrays of different dimensions and requires you to observe the following rules:

- The lower bound of any dimension in a C++ array is set at 0. You cannot override or alter this lower bound.

- Declaring a C++ array entails specifying the number of members in each dimension. Keep in mind that the upper bound is equal to the number of members, minus one! In the case of array aString, shown in the preceding syntax box, the range of valid array indices is 0 to 44.

- Declaring and using an array in an expression requires enclosing the array indices for each dimension in a separate set of square brackets.

Consider a simple program that uses arrays. Listing 6.3 contains the source code for program LST06_03.CPP. The program declares the array factorial to store the factorials of 0 to 8. The code uses a for loop to calculate the factorials for the elements at index 1 to 8. The program initializes the array element factorial[0] before the first for loop executes. Each loop iteration uses the factorial[i-1], gotten either from a previous loop iteration or from the pre-loop initialization. The program uses a second for loop (this one a downward-counting loop) to display the factorial values in array factorial.

Listing 6.3. The source code for the LST06_03.CPP program.

```
// LST06_03.CPP
// Program calculates a factorial using an array

#include <iostream.h>
#include <conio.h>

const MAX_FACTORIAL = 8;

main()
{
    double factorial[MAX_FACTORIAL + 1];
    int n;

    clrscr();
    // initialize array of factorials
    factorial[0] = 1;
    for (int i = 1; i <= MAX_FACTORIAL; i++)
      factorial[i] = i * factorial[i-1];

    for (i = MAX_FACTORIAL; i >= 0; i--)
      cout << i << "! = " << factorial[i] << "\n";
    getch();
    return 0;
}
```

Here is the output of the program in Listing 6.3:

```
8! = 40320
7! = 5040
6! = 720
5! = 120
4! = 24
3! = 6
2! = 2
1! = 1
0! = 1
```

C++ enables you to declare and initialize an array in one step. For example, the array `factorial` in Listing 6.3 can be explicitly initialized using the following statements (instead of using a loop):

```
double factorial[MAX_FACTORIAL + 1] = { 1, 1, 2, 6, 24, 120,
                                         720, 5040, 40320 }
```

The list of initializing values must contain a number of items that is equal to or less than the size of the array. If the list size is smaller than the array size, the C++ compiler assigns zeros to the trailing array elements that do not receive initializing values.

Another feature in C++ enables the size of an initializing list to determine the size of the initialized array. Here is how this feature can be applied to the array `factorial`:

```
double factorial[] = { 1, 1, 2, 6, 24, 120, 720, 5040, 40320 }
unsigned arraySize = sizeof(factorial) / sizeof(double);
```

The declaration for the variable `arraySize` stores the actual number of elements of array `factorial`. The number of array elements is calculated using the ratio of the total array's size (that is, `sizeof(factorial)`) to the size of the individual array element (that is, `sizeof(double)`). You can generalize this method to get the number of elements in any array that is declared and initialized in using a list of initial values.

Matrices

Matrices are two-dimensional arrays that use two indices to access their elements.

Two-Dimensional Arrays

The syntax for declaring a two-dimensional array is

```
type arrayName[numberOfRows][numberOfColumns];
```

Examples:

```
char Screen[25][80];
double dailyIncome[12][31];
```

Consider a simple example for using matrices. Listing 6.4 shows the source code for program LST06_04.CPP. The program performs the following tasks:

1. Declares the double-typed matrix mat with 10 rows and 3 columns.

2. Declares the double-typed array sumCol to have 3 elements.

3. Assigns random numbers to the elements of the matrix. This task uses a pair of nested for loops to iterate over the matrix rows and columns. The outer loop also assigns 0 to the various elements of array sumCol. The functions randomize() and random() are declared in the STDLIB.H header file. The function randomize() reseeds the random-number generator. The function random(n) returns random values in the range of 0 to n.

4. Adds the values of each matrix column in the elements of array sumCol. This task also uses a pair of nested for loops.

5. Displays the sums of columns that are stored in the array sumCol.

Listing 6.4. The source code for the LST06_04.CPP program.

```
// LST06_04.CPP
// Program demonstrates using matrices

#include <iostream.h>
#include <conio.h>
#include <stdlib.h>

const MAX_ROWS = 10;
const MAX_COLS =  3;

main()
{
    double mat[MAX_ROWS][MAX_COLS];
    double sumCol[MAX_COLS];

    clrscr();
    randomize();
    for (int row = 0; row < MAX_ROWS; row++)
      for (int col = 0; col < MAX_COLS; col++) {
        sumCol[col] = 0;
        mat[row][col] = random(1000) / (random(500) + 1);
      }
```

```
for (row = 0; row < MAX_ROWS; row++)
  for (col = 0; col < MAX_COLS; col++)
    sumCol[col] += mat[row][col];

for (col = 0; col < MAX_COLS; col++)
  cout << "Sum of column #" << col << " = "
       << sumCol[col] << "\n";
getch();
return 0;
}
```

Here is sample output generated by the program in Listing 6.4:

```
Sum of column #0 = 133
Sum of column #1 = 83
Sum of column #2 = 411
```

Because the program uses random numbers, it generates different results for each run.

Multi-Dimensional Array Storage

C++ also enables you to declare and initialize multi-dimensional arrays. The process is very similar to initializing a single-dimensional array. However, you need to know the rule of assigning values to a multi-dimensional array. This rule is based on how C++ stores the array elements. Consider a simple example of a matrix, Mat, with two rows and three columns. The sequence of storing the matrix elements is

```
Mat[0][0] Mat[0][1] Mat[0][2] Mat[1][0] Mat[1][1]  ...
```

Listing 6.5 contains the source code for program LST06_05.CPP. This program resembles that of Listing 6.4, except the double-typed matrix, mat, is assigned fixed values rather than random numbers. The program also uses an initializing list for the array sumCol. The other tasks performed by the program in Listing 6.5 resemble steps 4 and 5 that I mentioned in describing the tasks performed by the program in Listing 6.4.

Listing 6.5. The source code for the LST06_05.CPP program.

```
// LST06_05.CPP
// Program demonstrates using matrices

#include <iostream.n>
#include <conio.h>
```

continues

Listing 6.5. Continued

```
const MAX_ROWS = 2;
const MAX_COLS = 3;

main()
{
    double mat[MAX_ROWS][MAX_COLS] = { 1, 2 , 30,
                                       40, 500, 600 };
    double sumCol[MAX_COLS] = { 0, 0, 0 };

    clrscr();
    for (int row = 0; row < MAX_ROWS; row++)
      for (int col = 0; col < MAX_COLS; col++)
         sumCol[col] += mat[row][col];

   for (col = 0; col < MAX_COLS; col++)
     cout << "Sum of column #" << col << " = "
          << sumCol[col] << "\n";
     getch();
     return 0;
}
```

Here is the output generated by the program in Listing 6.5:

```
Sum of column #0 = 41
Sum of column #1 = 502
Sum of column #2 = 630
```

Using *for* loops To Create Open Loops

When I introduced the C++ for loop, I mentioned that the three components of the for loop are optional. In fact, C++ enables you to leave these three components empty! The result is an open loop. It is worthwhile to point out that other languages such as Ada and Modula-2 do support formal open loops and mechanisms to exit these loops. C++ enables you to exit from a loop in one of the following two ways:

- The break statement causes the program execution to resume after the end of the current loop. Use the break statement when you want to exit a for loop and resume with the remainder of the program. Turbo Pascal has no construct that resembles the break statement.

- The exit() function (declared in the STDLIB.H header file) enables you to exit the program. The exit() function works just like the Turbo Pascal HALT intrinsic. Use the exit() function if you want to stop iterating and also exit the program.

The next program uses an open loop to repeatedly prompt you for a number. The program takes your input and displays it along with its square value. Then the program asks whether you want to calculate the square of another number. If you type Y or y, the program performs another iteration. Otherwise, the program halts. As long as you keep typing Y or y for the latter prompt, the program keeps running (until the computer breaks down!). Listing 6.6 shows the source code for the LST06_06.CPP program.

Listing 6.6. The source code for the LST06_06.CPP program.

```
// LST06_06.CPP
// Program demonstrates using the for
// loop to emulate an infinite loop

#include <iostream.h>
#include <stdlib.h>
#include <conio.h>

main()
{
   char ch;
   double x, y;

   clrscr();
   // for loop with empty parts
   for (;;) {
      cout << "\n\nEnter a number: ";
      cin >> x;
      y = x * x;
      cout << "(" << x << ")^2 = " << y << "\n";
      cout << "More calculations? (Y/N) ";
      ch = getche();
      if (ch != 'y' && ch != 'Y')
         break;
   }
   return 0;
}
```

Here is a sample session with the program in Listing 6.6:

```
Enter a number: 5
(5)^2 = 25
More calculations? (Y/N) y

Enter a number: 7
(7)^2 = 49
More calculations? (Y/N) n
```

Skipping Loop Iterations

C++ enables you to skip to the end of a loop and resume the next iteration using the `continue` statement.

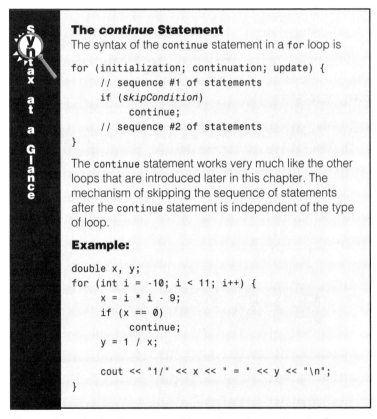

The *continue* Statement

The syntax of the `continue` statement in a `for` loop is

```
for (initialization; continuation; update) {
    // sequence #1 of statements
    if (skipCondition)
        continue;
    // sequence #2 of statements
}
```

The `continue` statement works very much like the other loops that are introduced later in this chapter. The mechanism of skipping the sequence of statements after the `continue` statement is independent of the type of loop.

Example:

```
double x, y;
for (int i = -10; i < 11; i++) {
    x = i * i - 9;
    if (x == 0)
        continue;
    y = 1 / x;

    cout << "1/" << x << " = " << y << "\n";
}
```

The `for` loop in the Syntax-at-a-Glance box shows that the first loop statement calculates the variable x using the value of the loop control variable i. The `if` statement determines whether x is 0 (this is true when i = -3 and +3). If this condition is true, the `if` statement informs the `continue` statement to skip the remaining two statements in the `for` loop.

Exiting Loops

C++ supports the `break` statement to exit a loop. The `break` statement makes the program resume after the end of the current loop.

The *break* Statement

The syntax of the break statement in a for loop is

```
for (initialization; continuation; update) {
      // sequence #1 of statements
      if (exitLoopCondition)
            break;
      // sequence #2 of statements
}
      // sequence #3 of statements
```

The break statement works very much like the other loops introduced later in this chapter. The mechanism for exiting a loop is independent of the type of loop.

Example:

```
char s[81], findChar;
// get string s and character for findChar
for (i = 0; i < strlen(s); i++)
      if (s[i] == findChar)
            break;
if (i < strlen(s))
      cout << "Found match at index "
            << i << "\n";
```

The example code in the Syntax-at-a-Glance box shows how an if statement inside a for loop may be used to search for a character in a string. While the for loop processes each character in the string, the if statement inside determines whether the character matches the character being searched (findChar). If a match is found, the break statement is executed and the for loop is terminated—control then passes to the if (i < strlen(s)) statement. The function strlen returns the length of its string argument and is declared in the STRING.H header file.

The *do-while* Loop

The do-while loop in C++ is a conditional loop that iterates as long as a condition is true. This condition is tested at the end of the loop. Therefore, the do-while loop iterates at least once.

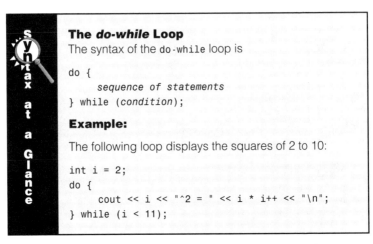

Consider a program that uses the do-while loop. Listing 6.7 contains the source code for the program LST06_07.CPP. The program performs the following tasks:

1. Prompts you to enter a string.

2. Converts your input into uppercase.

3. Displays the uppercase string.

4. Asks whether you want to enter another string. If you press the Y key, the program repeats the previous steps.

The program iterates as long as you press the Y key. The loop continuation test checks for your input being the lowercase or uppercase of the letter *Y.*

Listing 6.7. The source code for the LST06_07.CPP program.

```
// LST06_07.CPP
// Program demonstrates the do-while loop

#include <iostream.h>
#include <conio.h>
#include <string.h>

main()
```

```
{
    char c, aString[81];

    clrscr();
    do {
        cout << "Enter a string: ";
        cin.getline(aString, 80);
        strupr(aString);
        cout << aString << "\n"
             << "Enter another string? (Y/N) ";
        c = getche(); cout << "\n";
    } while (c == 'Y' || c == 'y');
    cout << "Press any key to end the program...";
    getch();
    return 0;
}
```

The function strupr converts the characters of its string argument into uppercase. The function is declared in the STRING.H header file. Here is a sample session with the program in Listing 6.7:

```
Enter a string: C++ is terrific
C++ IS TERRIFIC

Enter another string? (Y/N) n
Press any key to end the program...
```

The *while* Loop

C++'s while loop is another conditional loop that iterates as long as a condition is true. Thus, the while loop may never iterate if the tested condition is initially false.

Consider a program that uses the while loop. Listing 6.8 contains the source code for the program LST06_08.CPP. The program prompts you to enter a string and then uses a while loop to count the number of characters as well as the number of space characters in your input. The condition tested for iterating the while loop is the expression aString[i] == '\0'. This expression is true as long as the scanned character in your input string is not the null terminator.

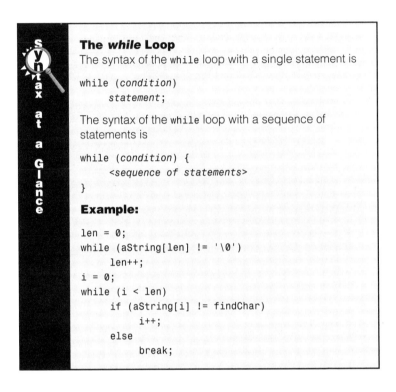

The *while* Loop

The syntax of the `while` loop with a single statement is

```
while (condition)
    statement;
```

The syntax of the `while` loop with a sequence of statements is

```
while (condition) {
    <sequence of statements>
}
```

Example:

```
len = 0;
while (aString[len] != '\0')
    len++;
i = 0;
while (i < len)
        if (aString[i] != findChar)
                i++;
        else
                break;
```

Listing 6.8. The source code for the LST06_08.CPP program.

```
// LST06_08.CPP
// Program demonstrates the while loop

#include <iostream.h>
#include <conio.h>

main()
{
   char aString[81];
   int i = 0, count = 0;

   clrscr();
   cout << "Enter a string: ";
   cin.getline(aString, 80);
   while (aString[i] != '\0') {
     if (aString[i] == ' ')
         count++;
     i++;
   }
```

```
    cout << "Your input is " << i - 1
         << " characters long and contains "
         << count << " spaces\n";
    getch();
    return 0;
}
```

Here is a sample session with the program in Listing 6.8:

```
Enter a string: C++ is the best language
Your input is 24 characters long and contains 4 spaces
```

Summary

This chapter covered the C++ loops and topics related to loops. You learned about the following subjects:

- The for loop, which contains three components: the loop initialization, the loop continuation condition, and the increment/decrement of the loop variables.

- Arrays, popular data structures that enable you to store a collection of indexable data items. C++ supports single-dimensional and multi-dimensional arrays. When you declare an array, you specify the number of elements in each dimension, enclosed in a separate set of brackets. C++ fixes the lower index for each dimension at 0. C++ also requires you to use separate sets of brackets for each array dimension when you use that array in an expression.

- Open loops, which are for loops with empty components. The break statement enables you to exit the current loop and resume program execution at the first statement that comes after the loop. The exit() function (declared in STDLIB.H) enables you to make a critical loop exit by halting the C++ program altogether.

- The continue statement, which enables you to jump to the end of the loop and resume with the next iteration. The advantage of the continue statement is that it does not require any labels to direct program execution.

- The do-while loop, which iterates at least once because its condition check is placed at the end of the loop.

- The while loop, which might not iterate because the condition is checked at the start of the loop. If the while loop's tested condition is initially false, it doesn't iterate.

Enumerated and Structured Data Types

The capability to create user-defined data types is among the features expected of modern programming languages. This chapter looks at the enumerated data types and structures that enable you to better organize your data. In this chapter, you learn about the following topics:

- Type definition using `typedef`

- Enumerated data types

- Structures

- Unions

Type Definition in C++

C++ offers the `typedef` keyword, which enables you to define new data type names as aliases of existing types.

typedef
The syntax of typedef is

typedef *knownType newType*;

Examples:

```
typedef unsigned word;
typedef unsigned char BOOLEAN;
typedef unsigned char BYTE;
```

The typedef defines a new type from a known one. You can use typedef to create aliases that shorten the names of existing data types. You can also use typedef to define the name of an array type.

Defining the Name of an Array Type
The syntax for defining the name of an array type is

typedef *baseType arrayTypeName*[*arraySize*];

The typedef statement defines the *arrayTypeName* with a basic type and size of *baseType* and *arraySize*, respectively.

Example:

```
typedef double realArray[10];
typedef double realMatrix[10][30];
main()
{
  realArray x; // declare array
  realMatrix mat; // declare matrix
  for (unsigned row = 0; row < 10; row++) {
    x[row] = 0;
    for (unsigned col = 0; col < 30; col++)
      mat[row][col] = (row != col) ? 1 : 0;
    }
    // other statements to manipulate the arrays
}
```

Enumerated Data Types

An enumerated type defines a list of unique identifiers and associates values with these identifiers. The rule to follow is that although the enumerated identifiers must be unique, the values assigned to them need not be.

Declaring an Enumerated Type
The syntax for declaring an enumerated type is

```
enum enumType { <enumeratedList> };
```

The *enumeratedList* is a list of enumerated identifiers.

Examples:

```
enum Boolean { false, true };
enum color { black, white, red,
             blue, green, yellow };
```

Here is another example of declaring an enumerated type:

```
enum diskCapacity { dsk360, dsk720, dsk1_2, dsk1_4, dsk2_8 };
```

C++ associates integer values with the enumerated identifiers. For example, in the preceding type, the compiler assigns 0 to dsk360, 1 to dsk720, and so on.

C++ is very flexible in declaring enumerated types. First, the language enables you to explicitly assign a value to an enumerated identifier. Here is an example:

```
enum weekDay { Sun = 1, Mon, Tue, Wed, Thu, Fri, Sat };
```

This declaration explicitly assigns 1 to the enumerated identifier Sun. The compiler then assigns the next integer, 2, to the next identifier, Mon, and so on. C++ enables you to explicitly assign a value to each member of the enumerated list. Moreover, these values need not be unique. Here are some examples of the flexibility of declaring enumerated types in C++:

```
// explicit value assignment for every list member
enum colors { black = 1, red = 2, blue = 3, green = 5,
              yellow = 7, white = 11 };

// intermittent value assignment
enum colors { black = 1, red, blue, green = 5,
              yellow = 7, white = 11 };
```

```
enum choiceType { false, true, dont_care = 0 };
```

In the last example, the compiler associates the identifier `false` with 0 by default. However, the compiler also associates the value 0 with `dont_care` because of the explicit assignment.

C++ enables you to declare variables that have enumerated types in the following ways:

■ The declaration of the enumerated type may include the declaration of the variables of that type. The syntax is

```
enum enumType { <list of enumerated identifiers> }
          <list of variables>;
```

Here is an example:

```
enum weekDay { Sun = 1, Mon, Tue, Wed, Thu, Fri, Sat }
          recycleDay, payDay, movieDay;
```

■ The enumerated type and its variables may be declared separately.

```
enum enumType { <list of enumerated identifiers> };
enumType var1, var2, ..., varN;
```

Consider an example. The program LST07_01.CPP, shown in Listing 7.1, uses an enumerated type to model the weekdays. The program prompts you to enter a number that corresponds to a weekday, and then it responds in the following ways:

■ If you enter 1 or 7 (to select Sunday or Saturday), the program displays the message `Oh! The weekend!`

■ If you enter 6 (to select Friday), the program displays the string `T.G.I.F.!!`

■ If you enter a number between 2 and 5, the program displays the message `Work, work, work!`

Listing 7.1. The source code for the LST07_01.CPP program.

```
// LST07_01.CPP
// Program demonstrates the use of enumerated types

#include <iostream.h>
#include <conio.h>

// make global enumerated definitions
enum WeekDays { NullDay, Sunday, Monday, Tuesday,
                Wednesday, Thursday, Friday, Saturday };
```

```
enum boolean { false, true };

main()
{
    WeekDays day;
    boolean more;
    char akey;
    unsigned j;

    clrscr();
    do {
        do {
          cout << "Enter a day number (Sun=1, Mon=2, etc.): ";
          cin >> j;
        } while (j < 1 || j > 7);
        day = WeekDay(NullDay + j);
        switch (day) {
            case Sunday:
            case Saturday:
                cout << "Oh! The weekend!";
                break;
            case Friday:
                cout << "T.G.I.F.!!";
                break;
            case Monday:
            case Tuesday:
            case Wednesday:
            case Thursday:
                cout << "Work, work, work!";
        }
        cout << "\nmore? (Y/N) ";
        akey = getche();
        more = (akey == 'Y' || akey == 'y') ? true : false;
        cout << "\n\n";
    } while (more == true);
    return 0;
}
```

The Turbo C++ program in Listing 7.1 uses the enumerated types
WeekDays and boolean. Here is a sample session from running that
program:

```
Enter a day number (Sun=1, Mon=2, etc.): 2
Work, work, work!
more? (Y/N) y

Enter a day number (Sun=1, Mon=2, etc.): 1
Oh! The weekend!
more? (Y/N) y

Enter a day number (Sun=1, Mon=2, etc.): 6
T.G.I.F.!!
more? (Y/N) n
```

Structures

C++ supports structures which enable you to define a new type that logically groups several fields or members. These members can be predefined types or other structures.

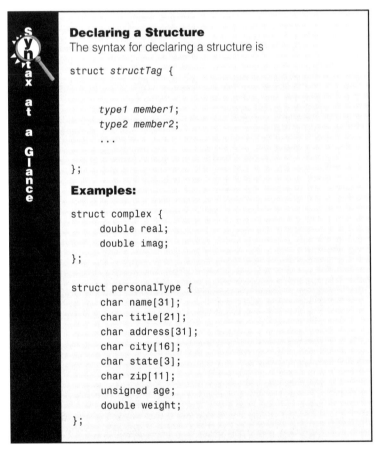

Declaring a Structure
The syntax for declaring a structure is

```
struct structTag {

    type1 member1;
    type2 member2;
    ...

};
```

Examples:

```
struct complex {
    double real;
    double imag;
};

struct personalType {
    char name[31];
    char title[21];
    char address[31];
    char city[16];
    char state[3];
    char zip[11];
    unsigned age;
    double weight;
};
```

After you define a `struct` type, you can use that type to declare variables. Here are examples of declarations that use structures declared in the preceding syntax box:

```
complex c1, c2, c3;
personalType me, you, dawgNamedBoo;
```

You can also declare structured variables when you define the structure itself, as shown here:

```
struct complex {
    double real;
    double imag;
} c1, c2, c3;
```

☞ Interestingly, C++ enables you to declare *untagged* structures (thus reducing name-space pollution). Using untagged structures involves declaring structure variables without defining a name for their structure. For example, the following structure definition declares the variables c1, c2, and c3 but omits the name of the structure:

```
struct {
    double real;
    double imag;
} c1, c2, c3;
```

C++ enables you to declare and initialize a structured variable. Here are two examples:

```
complex c = { 1.0, -8.3 };
personalType me = { "Namir Shammas", "author",
                    "4814 Mill Park", "Biscaine",
                    "MI", "48104", 38, 190.5 };
```

Use the dot operator to access the members of a structure. Here are a few examples:

```
c1.real = 12.45;
c1.imag = 34.56;
c2.real = 23.4 / c1.real;
c2.imag = 0.98 * c1.imag;
me.age = 38;
you.weight += 2; // gained 2 pounds!
```

Consider an example that uses simple structures and an array of structures. Listing 7.2 contains the source code for the LST07_02.CPP program. The program prompts you to enter four coordinates. The first three coordinates are reference values, and the fourth one is a search coordinate. The program calculates the closest and farthest reference coordinates from the search coordinate.

Listing 7.2. The source code for the LST07_02.CPP program.

```
// LST07_02.CPP
// Program demonstrates using structures

#include <iostream.h>
#include <conio.h>
```

continues

Listing 7.2. Continued

```
#include <math.h>

const int MAX_POINTS = 3;

struct TCoord {
    double X;
    double Y;
};

typedef TCoord TPoints[MAX_POINTS];

#define sqr(x) ((x) * (x))

main()
{
  TCoord Coord;
  TPoints Points;
  double MinDistance, MaxDistance, Distance;
  int i, Imax, Imin;

  clrscr();
  for (i = 0; i < MAX_POINTS; i++) {
    cout << "Enter X coordinate for point # " << i << ": ";
    cin >> Points[i].X;
    cout << "Enter Y coordinate for point # " << i << ": ";
    cin >> Points[i].Y; cout << "\n";
  }
  cout << "Enter X coordinate for search point: ";
  cin >> Coord.X;
  cout << "Enter Y coordinate for search point: ";
  cin >> Coord.Y; cout << "\n";
  // initialize the minimum distance variable with
  // a large value
  MinDistance = 1.0E+30;
  // initialize the maximum distance variable with a
  // negative value
  MaxDistance = -1.0;
  for (i = 0; i < MAX_POINTS; i++) {
    Distance = sqrt(sqr(Coord.X - Points[i].X) +
                    sqr(Coord.Y - Points[i].Y));
    // update minimum distance?
    if (Distance < MinDistance) {
      Imin = i;
      MinDistance = Distance;
    }
    // update maximum distance?
    if (Distance > MaxDistance) {
      Imax = i;
```

```
      MaxDistance = Distance;
    }
  }
  cout << "Point number " << Imin <<
          " is the closest to the search point\n"
       << "Point number " << Imax <<
          " is the farthest from the search point\n";
  getch();
  return 0;
}
```

The program accesses the X and Y members of structure TCoord using the expressions Coord.X and Coord.Y. Similarly, the program accesses the X and Y members of array Points using the expressions Points[i].X and Points[i].Y.

Here is a sample session with the program in Listing 7.2:

```
Enter X coordinate for point # 0: 1
Enter Y coordinate for point # 0: 1

Enter X coordinate for point # 1: 2
Enter Y coordinate for point # 1: 2

Enter X coordinate for point # 2: 3
Enter Y coordinate for point # 2: 3

Enter X coordinate for search point: 5
Enter Y coordinate for search point: 5

Point number 2 is the closest to the search point
Point number 0 is the farthest from the search point
```

Unions

Unions are special structures that store mutually exclusive members. The size of a union is equal to the size of its largest member.

Unions offer an easy alternative for quick data conversion. Unions were more significant in past decades, when the price of memory was much higher and consolidating memory using unions was feasible. Today's computers enjoy the abundance of inexpensive memory; thus, saving a few bytes here and there is a petty effort. Accessing union members involves the dot access operators, just as in structures.

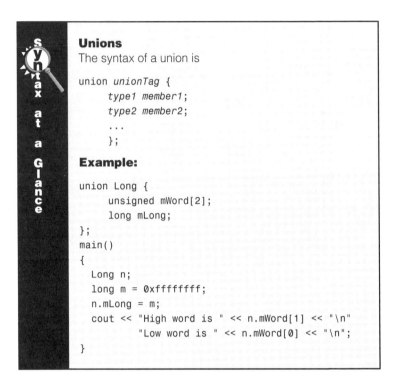

Summary

This chapter introduced user-defined data types and covered the following topics:

- The typedef statements, which enable you to create alias types of existing types and define array types.

- Enumerated data types, which enable you to declare unique identifiers that represent a collection of logically related constants.

- Structures, which enable you to define a new type that logically groups several fields or members. These members can be predefined types or other structures.

- Unions, which enable you to declare members that share a common memory block. By virtue of their storage scheme, unions enable you to save memory and perform automatic data conversion.

Pointers

Pointers are vital tools in C++. They enable you to access and process data quickly and efficiently. The success of C++ as a high-level language lies in how well it supports pointers. In this chapter, you learn about the following topics:

- Reference variables

- Pointers to simple variables

- Pointers to arrays

- Strings

- Pointers to structures

- Far pointers

Reference Variables

C++ supports a special type of association between variables, using reference variables. A reference variable becomes an alias for the variable it refers to. Reference variables are used in advanced classes and in the parameters of functions (you'll read more about this topic in the next chapter).

Declaring a Reference Variable
The syntax for declaring a reference variable is

```
type& referenceVar = variableName;
```

Example:

```
int x;

int& y = x;
```

The variable y is a reference (or an alias, if you prefer)
to variable x.

As an alias to the variables they refer to, reference variables can be
used to manipulate the original variables. Here is an example:

```
int x = 10;
int& y = x;
cout << "x = " << x << " and x (via ref. var.) = "
     << y << "\n";
y *= 2;
cout << "x = " << x << " and x (via ref. var.) = "
     << y << "\n";
```

The first output statement displays the following output:

```
x = 2 and x (via ref. var.) = 2
```

The statement that doubles the value of y also doubles the value of
x. The second output statement inspects the value stored in both
variables, x and y:

```
x = 4 and x (via ref. var.) = 4
```

Pointers to Simple Variables

In general terms, a *pointer* is a variable that stores an address of
another item, such as a variable, an array, a structure, a class, or a
function. C++ requires that you associate a data type (including
void) with a declared pointer. The associated data type can be a

predefined type or a user-defined structure. This association is needed to allow the pointer to properly interpret the data it's pointing to.

Declaring pointers in C++ is similar to declaring ordinary variables. The difference is that you need to place an asterisk before the name of the pointer.

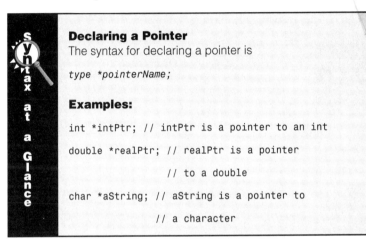

Declaring a Pointer
The syntax for declaring a pointer is

```
type *pointerName;
```

Examples:

```
int *intPtr; // intPtr is a pointer to an int

double *realPtr; // realPtr is a pointer

                 // to a double

char *aString; // aString is a pointer to

               // a character
```

C++ also enables you to declare nonpointers in the same lines that declare pointers, as shown here:

```
int *intPtr, anInt;
double *realPtr, x;
char *aString, aKey;
```

☞ C++ enables you to place the asterisk character right after the associated type. You should not interpret this kind of syntax to mean that every other identifier appearing on the same declaration line is automatically a pointer:

```
int* intPtr; // intPtr is a pointer to an int
double* realPtr; // realPtr is a pointer to a double
char* aString; // aString is a pointer to a character
int *intP, j; // intP is a pointer to int, j is an int
double *realPtr, *doublePtr; // both identifiers are
                             // pointers to a double
```

You need to initialize a pointer before you use it, just as with ordinary variables. In fact, the need to initialize pointers is more pressing—using uninitialized pointers invites trouble that leads to unpredictable program behavior or even a system hang!

C++ handles the dynamic allocation and deallocation of memory using the operators new and delete. The operator new returns the address of the dynamically allocated variable. The operator delete removes the dynamically allocated memory accessed by a pointer.

The *new* and *delete* Operators

The syntax for using the new and delete operators in creating dynamic scalar variables is

pointer = new *type*;

delete *pointer*;

Example:

```
int *p;

p = new int;

*p = 2;

cout << "Pointer p accesses the value " << *p

     << "\n";

delete p;
```

Allocating and Deallocating a Dynamic Array

The syntax for allocating and deallocating a dynamic array is

arrayPointer = new *type*[*arraySize*];

delete [] *arrayPointer*;

The *arrayPointer* is the pointer to a dynamic array.

Example:

```
double *dataPtr;

dataPtr = new double[10];

for (unsigned i = 0; i < 10; i++) {

    dataPtr[i] = (double) i;

    cout << "Element(" << i << ") = "

        << *(dataPtr + i) << "\n"

}

delete [] dataPtr;
```

☛ If the dynamic allocation of operator new fails, it returns a NULL (equivalent to 0) pointer. Therefore, to avoid potential trouble you need to test for a NULL pointer after using the new operator.

The Address-Of Operator &

To assign the address of a variable to a compatible pointer, you need to use the address-of operator &. The syntax of the address-of operator & is

pointer = &*variable*;

Example:

```
int x, *p;

p = &x; // p now stores the address of variable
x
```

8

The Reference Operator *

To access the contents of the memory location indicated by a pointer, you need to use the pointer reference operator *. The syntax of the reference operator * is

```
variable = *pointer;
```

Example:

```
int x = 10, y, *p;

p = &x; // p now stores the address of variable x

y = 2 + *p; // y now stores 12
```

Accessing Arrays with Pointers

A variable is simply a label that tags a memory address. Using a variable in a program means accessing the associated memory location by specifying its name (or tag, if you prefer). In this sense, a variable becomes a name that points to a memory location—in other words, a kind of pointer.

C++ supports a special use for the names of arrays. The compiler interprets the name of an array as the address of its first element. Thus, if x is an array, the expressions &x[0] and x are equivalent. In the case of a matrix—call it mat—the expressions &mat[0][0] and mat are also equivalent. This aspect of C++ makes it work as a high-level assembly language. When you have the address of a data item, you've got its number, so to speak. Knowing the memory address of a variable or an array enables you to manipulate its contents using pointers.

C++ enables you to use a pointer to access the various elements of an array. When you access the element x[i] of array x, the compiled code performs two tasks. First, it gets the base address of the array x (that is, where the first array element is located). Second, the compiled code uses the index i to calculate the offset from the base address of the array. This offset equals i multiplied by the size of the basic array type, as shown here:

```
address of element x[i] = address of x + i * sizeof(basicType)
```

Looking at this equation, assume that you have a pointer ptr that takes the base address of array x:

```
ptr = x; // pointer ptr points to address of x[0]
```

You can now substitute x with ptr in the equation and come up with the following equation:

```
address of element x[i] = ptr + i * sizeof(basicType)
```

C++ simplifies the use of this equation by absolving you from having to explicitly state the size of the basic array type. Thus, you can write the following equation:

```
address of element x[i] = p + i
```

This equation states that the address of element x[i] is the expression (p + i).

Consider an example for using pointers to access the elements of an array. Listing 8.1 contains the source code for program LST08_01.CPP. The program calculates factorials and stores them in an array. The program accesses the array elements using a pointer.

Listing 8.1. The source code for the program LST08_01.CPP.

```
// LST08_01.CPP
// Program calculates factorials using a pointer to an array

#include <iostream.h>
#include <conio.h>

const MAX_FACTORIAL = 4;

main()
{
    double factorial[MAX_FACTORIAL + 1];
    double *pArr = factorial;

    clrscr();
    // initialize array of factorials using the pointer pArr
    *pArr = 1;
    for (int i = 1; i <= MAX_FACTORIAL; i++)
      *(pArr + i) = i * pArr[i - 1];

    for (i = MAX_FACTORIAL; i >= 0; i--)
      cout << i << "! = " << *(pArr + i) << "\n";
    getch();
    return 0;
}
```

Notice that the program in Listing 8.1 uses the pointer pArr to access the elements of array factorial. The listing uses two forms for accessing an array element with a pointer. These two forms appear in the statement of the first for loop:

```
for (int i = 1; i <= MAX_FACTORIAL; i++)
  *(pArr + i) = i * pArr[i - 1];
```

The first form uses the expression *(pArr + i) to access the array element number i using the pointer pArr. The second form uses the expression pArr[i - 1] to access the array element number i-1 using the pointer pArr.

Here is the output of the program in Listing 8.1:

```
4! = 24
3! = 6
2! = 2
1! = 1
0! = 1
```

Strings

C++ treats strings as arrays of characters. The language uses the null character (ASCII 0) as an end-of-string indicator. This character is also called the *null terminator.* Every string must have a null terminator. Although C++ does not support string operators, it relies mostly on the string manipulation functions declared in the STRING.H header file, developed for C programmers. Table 8.1 lists the string manipulation functions in the STRING.H header file. Going over these functions in detail is beyond the scope of this book.

Table 8.1. The string manipulation functions in the STRING.H header file.

Function	Description
strcat()	Appends the contents of the source string to the target string.
strchr()	Examines the target string for the first occurrence of the pattern character.
strcmp()	Compares two strings.

Function	Description
strcpy()	Copies one string into another.
strcspn()	Scans a string and returns the length of the leftmost substring that totally lacks any character of a second string.
strdup()	Duplicates the string-typed argument.
stricmp()	Compares two strings without making a distinction between upper- and lowercase characters.
strlen()	Returns the length of a string.
strlwr()	Converts the uppercase characters of a string to lowercase.
strncat()	Appends, at most, a specified number of characters from the source string to the target string.
strncmp()	Compares a specified number of leading characters in two strings.
strncpy()	Copies a number of characters from the source string to the target string. Character truncation or padding can be performed, if necessary.
strnicmp()	Compares a specified number of leading characters in two strings, while ignoring the differences in the letter case.
strnset()	Overwrites a number of characters in a string with duplicate copies of a single character.
strrchr()	Searches a string for the last occurrence of the pattern character.
strrev()	Reverses the order of the string characters.
strset()	Replaces the contents of a string with the pattern character.
strspn()	Returns the number of characters in the leading part of the string that matches any character in the string pattern.
strstr()	Scans a string for the first occurrence of a substring.

continues

8

Table 8.1. Continued

Function	Description
strtod()	Converts a string into a double. String conversion is stopped when an unrecognizable character is scanned.
strtok()	Searches the target string for tokens. A string supplies the set of delimiter characters.
strtol()	Converts a string into a long integer. String conversion is stopped when an unrecognizable character is scanned. String image can be that of decimal, octal, and hexadecimal numbers.
strupr()	Converts the lowercase characters of a string into uppercase.

The C++ string libraries manipulate strings by using the pointers to the predefined type char. Listing 8.2 shows a string manipulating program. The program illustrates string input, copying, character conversion, and search.

Listing 8.2. The source code for the program LST08_02.CPP.

```
// LST08_02.CPP
// Program accesses a string using a pointer to char

#include <iostream.h>
#include <conio.h>
#include <string.h>

main()
{
    const STR_SIZE = 80;
    char String[STR_SIZE+1], subStr[STR_SIZE+1];
    char cStr[STR_SIZE+1], *p = String;

    clrscr();
    cout << "Enter a string: ";
    cin.getline(String, STR_SIZE);
    cout << "Enter search string: ";
    cin.getline(subStr, STR_SIZE);
    for (int count = 0; *p != '\0'; p++)
      count = (*p == ' ') ? count+1 : count;
```

```
        cout << "You entered " << (p - String) << " characters\n";
        cout << "You typed " << count << " spaces\n";
        strcpy(cStr, String);
        strupr(cStr);
        cout << "The uppercase of input string is: "
             << cStr << "\n";
        p = strstr(String, subStr);
        if (p) // same as if (p != NULL) {
          cout << "Substring match at index "
               << (p-String) << "\n";
        else
          cout << "No match for search string\n";
        getch();
        return 0;
}
```

The program in Listing 8.2 uses the getline() function to input a
string in the standard input stream, cin. The program counts both
the number of input characters and the number of spaces using a
for loop. This loop uses the character pointer, p, and the variable
count.

The pointer p is initialized by assigning it the address of the input
string, which is stored in variable String. The loop uses the
pointer p to access the characters of variable String—one character
per loop iteration. The loop increments the pointer p to access the
next character in variable String. The iteration stops when p points
to the null terminator character in variable String.

There is one statement in the loop that compares the accessed
character of variable String with the space character. If the two
items match, the statement increments the value in variable count.

After the loop ends, the program displays the number of input
characters. This value is taken as the difference between the addresses of pointers p (which now points to the null terminator in
the string of variable String) and String (remember that the name
of an array is also the pointer for its base address).

The program also uses the strcpy() function to copy the characters of variable String to the string cStr. Then the program converts the characters of variable cStr to uppercase, using the
function strupr().

Finally, the program finds the occurrence of the search string
(stored in variable subStr) in the variable String. The code uses
the function strstr() to return the pointer to the first matching
character stored in variable String. If no match is found, the

strstr() function returns NULL. The program uses an if statement
to determine whether the function strstr() found a match for the
search string. If the program found a match, it displays the index
of the main string where the search string appears. The program
calculates the value of this index as the difference between the
addresses of pointers p and String.

Here is a sample session with the program in Listing 8.2:

```
Enter a string: No strings attached!
Enter search string: string
You entered 20 characters
You typed 2 spaces
The uppercase of input string is: NO STRINGS ATTACHED!
Substring match at index 3
```

Pointers to Structures

Assigning the address of a struct variable to a pointer uses the
same syntax as that for simple variables, whereas accessing the
members of the structure requires the -> operator. This operator
enables the pointer to the structure to specify a particular structure member.

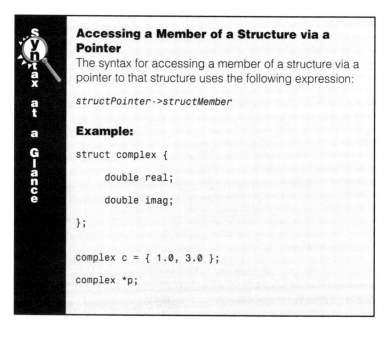

Syntax at a Glance

Accessing a Member of a Structure via a Pointer

The syntax for accessing a member of a structure via a
pointer to that structure uses the following expression:

structPointer->structMember

Example:

```
struct complex {

      double real;

      double imag;

};


complex c = { 1.0, 3.0 };

complex *p;
```

```
p = &c; // assign the address of c to pointer p

// access the members of c using p->real

// and p->imag

cout << "c = " << p->real << " +i "

        << p->imag << "\n";
```

Consider a program that illustrates accessing the members of a structured variable as well as an array of structures. Listing 8.3 shows the source code for the program LST08_03.CPP. The program internally assigns values to an array of structures that model the coordinates of two-dimensional points. The program then calculates and displays the center of the array of points.

Listing 8.3. The source code for the program LST08_03.CPP.

```
// LST08_03.CPP
// Program demonstrates using pointers to structures

#include <iostream.h>
#include <conio.h>

const int MAX_POINTS = 3;

struct TCoord {
    double X;
    double Y;
};

typedef TCoord TPoints[MAX_POINTS];

main()
{
  TCoord Coord = { 0, 0 }, *pCoord = &Coord;
  TPoints Points = { { 1.5, 1.7 }, { 2.2, 2.8 },
                     { 3.2, 3.9 } };
  TPoints *pPoints = &Points;
  clrscr();
  for (int i = 0; i < MAX_POINTS; i++) {
    pCoord->X += (*pPoints+i)->X;
    pCoord->Y += (*pPoints+i)->Y;
  }
  pCoord->X /= MAX_POINTS;
  pCoord->Y /= MAX_POINTS;
  cout << "Center point is at (" << pCoord->X
```

continues

Listing 8.3. Continued

```
       << ", " << pCoord->Y << ")\n";
  getch();
  return 0;
}
```

The program in Listing 8.3 declares the structure TCoord and the array of structures TPoints. The program uses the pointers pCoord and pPoints to access members of structures Coord and Points, respectively. The program utilizes the expressions pCoord->X and pCoord->Y to access the X and Y members of the structure TCoord, respectively. Similarly, the program employs the expressions (*pPoints+i)->X and (*pPoints+i)->Y to access the X and Y members of an element in array Points.

Far Pointers

The architecture of the Intel 80x86 processors uses 64K segments. This means that the pointers used so far store the offset address to only the currently used 64K data segment. What happens when you need to access an address that lies outside the current data segment? You need to use *far* pointers. Such pointers store both the segment and offset addresses of a memory location and consequently require more memory. That is why not every C++ pointer is a far pointer.

To declare a pointer as far, you need to place the keyword far between the pointer's access type and its name.

Declaring a *far* Pointer
The syntax for declaring a far pointer is

type far **farPointer*;

Example:

int far *screenPtr = (int far *) 0xB8000000;

To use a far pointer, you need to assign it a far-typed address:

```
farPointer = (type far *) address;
```

Consider a simple example. Listing 8.4 shows the source code for the LST08_04.CPP program. The program writes directly to the color video (I am assuming that you have a color video adapter!) and fills the screen with the letter you type. The program fills the screen with a different letter, using a different color, until you press the letter *Q*.

Listing 8.4 shows the declaration of the VIDEO_ADDR macro that stores the long-typed address 0xB8000000, the base address of the color video adapter. The program declares the pointer screenPtr in the following way:

```
int far *screenPtr;
```

The program assigns the base address of the adapter to the screenPtr pointer using the following statement:

```
screenPtr = (int far *) VIDEO_ADDR;
```

Then the following statement enables the screenPtr pointer to write directly to the screen:

```
*(screenPtr + i) = ch ¦ attr;
```

Listing 8.4. The source code for the LST08_04.CPP program.

```cpp
// LST08_04.cpp
// Program uses a far pointer to write directly
// to a color video screen

#include <iostream.h>
#include <conio.h>

#define VIDEO_ADDR 0xB8000000 // address of a color monitor
#define DISPLAY_ATTR 0x0100

main()
{
  int far *screenPtr;
  long attr = DISPLAY_ATTR;
  const int BYTES = 2000;
  char ch;

  clrscr();
  cout << "Press any key (Q to exit)";
```

```
while ((ch = getche()) != 'Q') {
    clrscr();
    screenPtr = (int far *) VIDEO_ADDR;
    for (int i = 0; i < BYTES; i++)
        *(screenPtr + i) = ch | attr;
    attr += 0x0100;
}
}
```

Summary

This chapter introduced pointers and covered the following topics:

■ Reference variables create aliases for existing variables. Manipulating a reference variable also changes the reference variable.

■ Pointers to simple variables offer hooks that enable you to access variables.

■ Pointers to arrays are powerful tools that enable your programs to access the various array elements.

■ C++ enables you to use the name of an array as the pointer to its first member. Thus if arrayVar is an array, the name arrayVar and &arrayVar[0] are equivalent.

■ Strings are arrays of characters that end with the null character. C++ inherits string-manipulating libraries from C. These libraries manipulate strings using pointers to the type char.

■ Pointers to structures use the -> operator to access the various members of a structure.

■ Far pointers empower your application to access data that lies outside the current data segment.

■ To use a far pointer, you need to assign it a far-typed address.

Functions

Functions are the basic building blocks that conceptually extend the C++ language to fit your custom applications. C, the parent language of C++, is more function-oriented than C++. This difference is due to C++'s support of classes, inheritance, and other object-oriented programming features. Nevertheless, functions play an important role in C++. In this chapter, you learn about the following aspects of simple C++ functions:

- Function syntax

- Prototyping functions

- `inline` functions

- Using `void` functions as procedures

- Recursive functions

- Exiting functions

- Default arguments for a function's parameters

- Overloading functions

- Passing variables by reference

- Passing arrays as function arguments

- Passing strings as function arguments

- Passing structures as function arguments

- Accessing the command-line arguments

- Pointers to functions

Function Syntax

Functions are essential building blocks in C++. They extend the language in ways tailored to specific applications. In addition, functions support structured programming techniques because they are highly independent program components. Every C++ program must have the function main(). The programs presented so far make function main() return an integer value, typically 0. In this respect, the function main() behaves like an ordinary function. Also included in the programs you've seen so far are many pre-defined functions. Now it's time to explore functions you can define to accommodate your C++ applications.

Declaring Functions
The syntax of the ANSI C style of declaring functions (which C++ adheres to) is

returnType functionName(parameterList)

The *parameterList* is a comma-delimited list of parameters that states the data type and the name of each parameter.

Examples:

```
double square(double x)
{ return x * x; }
char toUpCase(char c)
{ return (c >= 'a' && c <= 'z') ? c-'a'+'A' : c;}
```

Notice the following aspects of C++ functions:

- The return type of the C++ function appears before the function's name.

- If the parameter list is empty, you still use empty parentheses. C++ also enables you to optionally use the void keyword to explicitly state that the parameter list is void.

- The typed parameter list consists of a list of typed parameters that use the following format:

  type1 parameter1, type2 parameter2, ...

  This format shows that the individual parameter is declared just like a variable—you state the type first and then the parameter's identifier. The list of parameters in C++ is comma delimited. In addition, you *cannot* group a sequence of parameters that have exactly the same data type. You must declare each parameter explicitly.

■ The body of a C++ function is enclosed in an open brace ({) and a close brace (}). There is no semicolon after the closing brace.

■ C++ supports passing parameters by value and by reference, which you will learn about in the following sections.

■ C++ supports local constants, data types, and variables. Although these data items can appear in nested block statements, C++ does not support nested functions.

■ The `return` keyword returns the function's value.

Prototyping Functions

C++ requires you to either declare or define a function before using it. Declaring a function, commonly called *prototyping,* lists the function name, the return type, and the number and type of its parameters. Including the name of the parameters is optional. You also need to place a semicolon after the close parenthesis. C++ requires that you declare a function if you call the function before you define it. Here is a simple example:

```
// prototype the function square
double square(double);

main()
{
  cout << "4.5^2 = " << square(4.5) << "\n";
  return 0;
}

double square(double x)
{ return x * x; }
```

Notice that the declaration of function `square()` does not include the name of its single parameter.

Typically, the declaration of a function is global. You can still prototype a function inside its client function. This approach hides the prototype from other functions. Consequently, other functions cannot call the prototype function unless they are declared after the declaration of the prototyped function.

inline Functions

Using functions incurs the overhead of calling them, passing their arguments, and returning their results. C++ enables you to use inline *functions* that expand, much like a macro, into a set of pre-defined statements. Thus, inline functions offer faster execution speed (especially where speed is critical) at the cost of expanding the code.

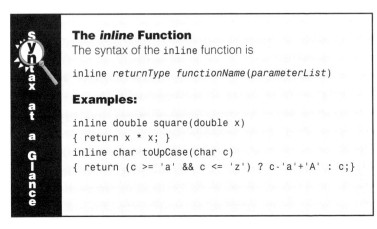

The *inline* Function
The syntax of the inline function is

```
inline returnType functionName(parameterList)
```

Examples:

```
inline double square(double x)
{ return x * x; }
inline char toUpCase(char c)
{ return (c >= 'a' && c <= 'z') ? c-'a'+'A' : c;}
```

The alternative to using inline functions is to use the #define directive to create macro-based pseudofunctions. Many C++ programmers highly recommend abandoning this method in favor of inline functions. The reason for this bias is that inline functions offer type checking, which is totally lacking when you use macros created with the #define directive.

Void Functions as Procedures

The ANSI C standard recognizes the type void as typeless. Consequently, the void type enables you to create a form of a procedure which is merely a function that returns a void type. The C++ ANSI committee has adopted the ANSI C standard in supporting and using the void type. Before the advent of the void type in C, programmers declared the return type to be int and simply discarded the function result by placing the function call in a statement by itself. Some C programmers use the #define directive to create void as an alias to int.

Here are some simple examples of `void` functions that clear the
screen and move the cursor (these functions require that the
ANSI.SYS driver, or compatible, be installed in your CONFIG.SYS
file):

```
void clrscr()
{ cout << "\x1b[2J"; }

void gotoxy(int col, int row)
{ cout << "\x1b[" << row << ";" << col << "H"; }

void clreol()
{ cout << "\x1b[K"; }
```

Recursive Functions

C++ supports *recursive* functions, which are functions that call
themselves. There is no need for a special syntax to indicate that
the function is recursive. Following is a simple example that calculates a factorial using recursion. The function `factorial()` returns
the factorial of the parameter x by recursively calling itself:

```
double factorial(int x)
// recursive factorial function
{ return (x > 1) ? (double) x * factorial(x - 1) : 1.0; }
```

Exiting Functions

Frequently, you make an early exit from a routine because certain
conditions do not enable you to continue executing the statements
in that routine. C++ provides the `return` statement to exit from a
function. If the function has the `void` type (that is, the function
does not return a value), you employ the statement `return;` and
include no expression after the `return` keyword. By contrast, if you
exit a non-`void` function, your `return` statement should yield a
value that indicates the reason for exiting the function. Here is an
example:

```
double factorial(int n)
{
   double product = 1;
   if (n < 2)
      return product;
   for (int i = 2; i <= n; i++)
     product *= (double) i;
   return product;
}
```

Default Arguments

A default argument is a new language feature that is quite simple
and yet very powerful. C++ enables you to assign default arguments to the parameters of a function. When you omit the argument of a parameter that has a default argument, the default
argument is automatically used. Using default arguments requires
that you follow these rules:

1. After you assign a default argument to a parameter, you must
   do so for all subsequent parameters in the same parameter list. You cannot randomly assign default arguments
   to parameters. This rule means that the parameter list can be
   divided into two groups: the leading parameters do not
   have default arguments, whereas the trailing parameters do.

2. In the calling routine, you must supply an argument for each
   parameter that has no default argument.

3. In the calling routine, you may omit the argument for a
   parameter that has a default argument.

4. After you omit the argument for a parameter with a default
   argument, the arguments for all subsequent parameters must
   be omitted.

☛   The best way to list the parameters with default arguments is
by placing parameters according to the likelihood of using their
default arguments. Place the least-likely-used arguments first and
the most-likely-used arguments last.

Here is a simple example that shows the use of default arguments:

```
double power(double base,
             double exponent = 2,
             double errorValue = -1.E+30)
{ return (base > 0) ? exp(exponent * log(base)) : errorValue;}
```

The function power() raises a number to a power. The parameters
of the function are base, exponent, and errorValue. The base parameter represents the base number and has no default argument.
The exponent parameter represents the power to which the base
number is raised. The exponent parameter has the default argument of 2. The parameter errorValue represents the numeric code
for an error that results due to using a nonpositive argument for
the base number. The default argument for the errorValue parameter is –1.E+30, a large negative number.

Here are sample calls to function `power()`:

```
z1 = power(x, y, -1.0E+300);
z2 = power(x, y);
z3 = power(x);
```

The first call to function `power()` passes arguments to all the function's parameters. The second call omits the argument for the last parameter. Consequently, the compiler assigns the default argument of $-1.E+30$ to the `errorValue` parameter. The third call uses the default arguments for the second and third parameters. Thus, the compiler assigns the default arguments of 2 and $-1.E+30$ to the parameters `exponent` and `errorValue`, respectively.

Function Overloading

Function overloading is a language feature in C++ that has no parallel in C, Pascal, or Modula-2. This new feature enables you to declare multiple functions that have the same name but different parameter lists (a parameter list is also called the function *signature*). The function's return type is not part of the function signature, because C++ enables you to discard the result type. Consequently, the compiler cannot distinguish between two functions with the same parameters and different return types when these return types are omitted.

CAUTION

Using default arguments with overloaded functions might end up duplicating the signature for some of the functions (when the default arguments are used). The C++ compiler can detect this ambiguity and generate a compile-time error.

The next example shows three overloaded `power()` functions:

```
double power(double base, double exponent)
{ return (base > 0) ? exp(exponent * log(base)) : -1.E+30; }

double power(double base, int exponent)
{
  double product = 1;
  if (exponent > 0)
    for (unsigned i = 1; i <= exponent; i++)
      product *= base;
  else
```

```
    for (unsigned i = -1; i >= exponent; i--)
       product /= base;
  return product;
}

long power(int base, int exponent)
{
  long product = 1;
  if (base > 0 && exponent > 0)
    for (unsigned i = 1; i <= exponent; i++)
       product *= base;
  else
    product = -0xffffffff;
  return product;
}
```

The first overloaded function raises a double-typed base number to a double-typed exponent and yields a double-typed return. The second overloaded function raises a double-typed base number to an int-typed exponent and yields a double-typed return. The third overloaded function raises an int-typed base number to an int-typed exponent and yields a long-typed return. The overloaded functions are distinctly coded. Each version takes advantage of the parameter types.

Here are some sample calls to the overloaded function power():

```
double x = 2, y = 3, z;
int b = 2, e = 3;
long a;
z = power(x, y); // call power(double, double)
z = power(x, e); // call power(double, int)
a = power(b, e); // call power(int, int);
```

The first call to function power() passes the double-typed arguments x and y. Consequently, the compiler resolves this call by using the power(double, double) version. The second call to function power() passes the double-typed variable x and int-typed variable e. Therefore, the compiler resolves this call by using the power(double, int) version. The last call to function power() passes int-typed variables b and e. Consequently, the compiler resolves this call by using the power(int, int) version.

Passing Arrays as Arguments

When you write a C++ function that passes an array as a parameter, you need to declare that parameter as a pointer to the basic type of the array.

Prototyping a Function with an Array Parameter

The syntax for prototyping such a function is

```
basicType array;
returnType function(basicType*,
                    <other parameter types>);
```

The syntax for defining the preceding function is

```
returnType function(basicType *arrParam,
                    <other parameters>)
```

or

```
returnType function(basicType arrParam[],
                    <other parameters>)
```

Examples:

```
// prototypes
void ShellSort(unsigned *intArray,
               unsigned arraySize);
void QuickSort(unsigned intArray[],
               unsigned arraySize);
```

C++ enables you to declare the array parameter using a pair of empty brackets. C++ programmers use this form less frequently than the explicit pointer form, even though the brackets actually enhance the code readability.

Here is a code fragment that shows an array of integers being passed to a sort() function:

```
main()
{
    int intArr[] = { 6, 4, 3, 7, 8, 1, 2, 9, 5, 10 };
    int arrSize = sizeof(intArr) / sizeof(int);
    void sort(int*, int); // prototype the function sort
    sort(intArr, arrSize); // call the function sort
    for (unsigned i = 0; i < arrSize; i++)
        cout << intArr[i] << " ";
    return 0;
}

void sort(int array[], int numElem)
{
    // statements to sort the array
}
```

Using Strings as Arguments

Because C++ treats strings as arrays of characters, the rules for
passing arrays as arguments to functions also apply to strings. Here
is a simple example for a string function that converts the characters of its arguments to uppercase:

```
char* uppercase(char* string)
{
   int ascii_shift = 'A' - 'a';
   char* strptr = string;

   // loop to convert each character to uppercase
   while ( *strptr != '\0') {
       if ((*strptr  >= 'a' && *strptr <= 'z'))
           *strptr += ascii_shift;
       strptr++;
   }
   return string;
}
```

The function assigns the address in the parameter string to the
local pointer strptr. The function then uses the local pointer to
process the characters of the string parameter. Finally, the function returns the pointer string, which still stores the base address
of the client string.

Using Structures as Arguments

C++ enables you to pass structures either by value or by reference. This section demonstrates passing structures by value. The
next section shows you how to pass structures by reference. The
structure's type appears in the function prototype and heading in a
manner similar to that of predefined types.

```
#include <iostream.h>
struct TPoint {
    double x;
    double y;
};

// prototype function
TPoint getMidPoint(TPoint, TPoint);

main()
{
    TPoint pt1 = { 1, 1 };
    TPoint pt2 = { 2, 2 };
    TPoint m = getMidPoint(pt1, pt2);
    cout << "Mid point is (" << m.x << ", " << m.y << ")\n";
```

```
        return 0;
}
TPoint getMidPoint(TPoint p1, TPoint p2)
{
        TPoint result;
        result.x = (p1.x + p2.x) / 2;
        result.y = (p1.y + p2.y) / 2;
        return result;
};
```

The call to function `getMidPoint()` passes copies of the structured variables `pt1` and `pt2`. The function `getMidPoint()` works with the copies.

Passing Arguments by Reference

Normally, C++ functions pass arguments by value, submitting *copies* of the original data to the functions. The functions can change the values within them without affecting the original data, which is located outside the scope of the function. C++ enables you to write functions with parameters that pass arguments by reference. Using this kind of parameter, you can change the value of the argument beyond the scope of the function. C++ offers two ways to implement such parameters: pointers and formal reference parameters. The following subsections present functions that pass various kinds of data types by reference.

Passing Simple Variables

You can pass pointers or references to simple variables to a function in order to alter the value of these variables beyond the scope of the function. Here is a function that swaps two integers by passing pointers to the type `int`:

```
void swap(int* pi, int* pj)
{
  int temp = *pi;
  *pi = *pj;
  *pj = temp;
}
```

The `swap()` function uses the expressions `*pi` and `*pj` to access the integers referenced by the addresses of the `int` variables `i` and `j` in this sample call:

```
int i = 2, j = 90;
cout << "i = " << i << " and j = " << j << "\n";
swap(&i, &j);
cout << "i = " << i << " and j = " << j << "\n";
```

The call to function swap() must pass the addresses of the swapped variables.

Here is the version of function swap() that uses formal references:

```
void swap(int& ri, int& rj)
{
  int temp = ri;
  ri = rj;
  rj = temp;
}
```

The parameters ri and rj are reference parameters. Therefore, these parameters become temporary aliases to their arguments within the scope of function swap(). Consequently, any changes made to the parameters ri and rj also affect their arguments beyond the scope of the function swap(). Also notice that the function uses the parameters without any special access operators. Here is a sample call to function swap():

```
int i = 2, j = 90;
cout << "i = " << i << " and j = " << j << "\n";
swap(i, j);
cout << "i = " << i << " and j = " << j << "\n";
```

The call to function swap() simply passes the swapped variables, i and j.

Passing Structures by Reference

You can pass structures to functions by using either pointers or formal reference. Many C++ programmers consider either approach as more efficient than passing the structure parameters by value—you save on the overhead of copying the structure.

Here is a version of the code fragment that uses function getMidPoint() and passes its parameters by using pointers and references:

```
#include <iostream.h>
struct TPoint {
    double x;
    double y;
};

// prototype function
void getMidPoint(TPoint*, TPoint*, TPoint&);

main()
{
    TPoint pt1 = { 1, 1 };
    TPoint pt2 = { 2, 2 };
```

```
        TPoint m;
        getMidPoint(&pt1, &pt2, m);
        cout << "Mid point is (" << m.x << ", " << m.y << ")\n";
        return 0;
}

void getMidPoint(TPoint* p1, TPoint* p2, TPoint& mp)
{
        mp.x = (p1->x + p2->x) / 2;
        mp.y = (p1->y + p2->y) / 2;
};
```

The new version of function getMidPoint() returns its result using the third parameter, mp, which is a reference parameter. The first two function parameters are pointers to TPoint structures. Thus, the reference parameter serves in this case to get information from the called function. In practice, reference parameters that return values are suitable when a function returns multiple results.

Passing Pointers to Dynamic Structures

The binary tree is among the popular dynamic data structures. Such structures empower you to build ordered collections of data without prior knowledge of the number of data items. The basic building block for a binary tree is a node. Each node has a field that is used as a sorting key, optional additional data (called *non-key data*), and two pointers to establish a link with other tree nodes. Dynamic memory allocation enables you to create space for each node and to dynamically set up the links between the various nodes. To learn more about binary tree structure, consult a data structure textbook.

Implementing a binary tree requires functions that, at least, insert, search, delete, and traverse the tree. All of these functions access the binary tree through the pointer of its root. Interestingly, operations such as tree insertion and deletion can affect the root itself. In such cases, the address of the root node changes. Consequently, you need to pass a reference to the pointer of the root node, *not just* the pointer to the root node. Using a reference to a pointer guarantees that you maintain an updated address of the tree root. Here is sample code for the function that inserts unsigned integers in a binary tree:

```
typedef unsigned int word;
typedef struct node* nodeptr;

struct node {
   word value;
   nodeptr left;
```

```
    nodeptr right;
};

void insert(nodeptr& root, word item)
// recursively insert element in binary tree
{
    if (!root)  {
        root = new node;
        root->value = item;
        root->left = NULL;
        root->right = NULL;
    }
    else {
        if (item < root->value)
            insert(root->left,item);
        else
            insert(root->right,item);
    }
}
```

Notice that the first parameter of function insert() is a reference
to the tree node pointer type, nodeptr. This kind of parameter ensures that when you insert the first item in the tree, you get the
updated address of pointer root. Initial insertion alters the value of
this pointer from NULL to the memory address of the tree root.
When you deal with more complex versions of the binary tree,
such as the AVL tree, the red-black tree, and the splay tree, passing
the reference to the root pointer is even more critical. This is because these trees often rearrange their nodes and select a new tree
root.

Accessing Command-Line Arguments

C++ enables you to access command-line arguments by supplying
and using the following parameters in function main():

```
main(int argc, char* argv[])
```

The argc parameter returns the number of command-line arguments. The argv parameter is a character pointer that accesses the
various command-line arguments. The value of argc takes into ac-
count the name of the program itself. The expression argv[0] is
the pointer to the program's name. The expression argv[1] is a
pointer to the first command-line argument, and so on.

Here is a simple code fragment that displays the name of the program and the command-line arguments:

```
#include <iostream.h>

main(int argc, char* argv[])
{
  cout << "Program name is " << argv[0] << "\n";
  for (int i = 1; i < argc; i++)
    cout << "Argument number #" << i << " is "
    << argv[i] << "\n";
  return 0;
}
```

Pointers to Functions

The program compilation process translates the names of variables into memory addresses where data is stored and retrieved. Pointers to addresses can also access these addresses. This translation step holds true for variables and functions alike. The compiler translates the name of a function into the address of executable code. C++ extends the strategy of manipulating variables by using pointers to functions.

Syntax at a Glance

Declaring a Pointer to a Function
The syntax for declaring a pointer to a function is

```
returnType (*functionPointer)(parameterList);
```

This form tells the compiler that the *functionPointer* is a pointer to a function that has the *returnType* return type and a list of parameters.

Examples:

```
double (*fx)(double x);
void (*sort)(int* intArray, unsigned n);
unsigned (*search)(int searchKey, int* intArray,
                   unsigned n);
```

The first identifier, fx, points to a function that returns a double and has a single double-typed parameter. The second identifier, sort, is a pointer to a function that returns a void type and takes two parameters: a pointer to int and an unsigned. The third identifier, search, is a pointer to a function that returns an unsigned and has three parameters: an int, a pointer to an int, and an unsigned.

Declaring an Array of Function Pointers
C++ enables you to declare an array of function pointers. The syntax is

```
returnType (*functionPointer[arraySize])
          (parameterList);
```

Examples:

```
double (*fx[3])(double x);
void (*sort[MAX_SORT])(int* intArray,
                       unsigned n);
unsigned (*search[MAX_SEARCH])(int searchKey,
                               int* intArray,
                               unsigned n);
```

The first example in the syntax box declares the array of three function pointers, fx. Each member of array fx points to a function that returns the double type and has a single double-typed parameter. The second example declares the array of MAX_SORT function pointers, sort. Each member of the array sort points to a function that has the void return type and takes two parameters: a pointer to an int (which is the pointer to an array of integers) and an unsigned (the number of array members to sort). The third example declares an array of MAX_SEARCH function pointers, search. Each member of the array search points to a function that returns an unsigned value and has three parameters: an int (the search value), a pointer to int (pointer to the searched array of integers), and an unsigned (the number of array members to search).

As with any pointer, you need to initialize a function pointer before using it. This step is simple: you merely assign the bare name of a function to the function pointer.

Initializing a Pointer to a Function
The syntax for initializing a pointer to a function is

```
functionPointer = aFunction;
```

The assigned function must have the same return type and parameter list as the function pointer. Otherwise, the compiler flags an error.

Example:

```
void (*sort)(int* intArray, unsigned n);
sort = qsort;
```

Assigning a Function to an Array of Function Pointers
The syntax for assigning a function to an element in an array of function pointers is

```
functionPointer[index] = aFunction;
```

After you assign a function name to a function pointer, you can use the pointer to invoke its associated function. Now it should become evident why the function pointer must have the same return type and parameter list as the accessed function.

Example:

```
void (*sort[2])(int* intArray, unsigned n);
sort[0] = qsort;
sort[1] = shellSort;
```

Invoking Function Pointers
The syntax of the expression that invokes function pointers is

```
(*functionPointer)(<argument list>);
(*functionPointer[index])(<argument list>);
```

Example:

```
(*sort)(&intArray, n);
(*sort[0])(&intArray, n);
```

Here is a code fragment for a pointer to a function:

```
double square(double x)
{ return x * x; }

main()
{
  // declare the function pointer
  double (*sqr)(double);

  sqr = square; // assign function to function pointer
  cout << "5 squared = " << (*sqr)(5.0) << "\n";
  return 0;
}
```

The code assigns the address of function `square()` to the function pointer `sqr`. The code then invokes the function `square()` using the pointer `sqr`.

Summary

This chapter presented simple C++ functions. You learned about the following topics:

- The general form for defining functions is

```
returnType functionName(parameterList)
{
<declarations of data items>

<function body>
return returnValue;
}
```

- The `inline` functions enable you to expand their statements in place, like macro-based pseudofunctions. However, unlike these pseudofunctions, `inline` functions perform type checking.

- The `void` functions are routines that perform a task and return no result.

- Recursive functions perform an iterative task by calling themselves.

- Exiting C++ functions takes place using the `return` statement. The `void` functions need not include an expression after the `return` keyword.

- Default arguments enable you to assign default values to the parameters of a function. When you omit the argument of a parameter that has a default argument, that default argument is automatically used.

- Function overloading enables you to declare multiple functions that have the same name but different parameter lists (also called the function signature). The function's return type is not part of the function signature, because C++ enables you to discard the result type.

- Passing arrays as function arguments involves using pointers to the basic types. C++ enables you to declare array parameters using explicit pointer types or using the empty brackets. Such parameters enable you to write general-purpose functions that work with arrays of different sizes. In addition, these pointers access the array by using its address, instead of making a copy of the entire array.

■ Passing structures as function arguments enables you to shorten the parameter list by encapsulating various related information in C++ structures.

■ When passing reference parameters, you can use pointers or formal references. The formal references become aliases of their arguments. In the case of passing reference to pointers, such reference can update the address of the argument.

■ Accessing the command-line arguments involves using special parameters in function main(). These parameters get the number of command-line arguments as well as a pointer to each command-line argument.

■ Pointers to functions are valuable tools that enable you to indirectly invoke a function. In fact, using parameters that include pointers to functions enables you to create libraries that can be used with functions not yet written.

Building Classes

Classes provide C++ with object-oriented programming constructs. This chapter introduces building classes. The next chapter offers more advanced topics related to classes and object-oriented programming. This chapter covers the following topics:

- Basics of object-oriented programming
- Declaring base classes
- Constructors
- Destructors
- Static members
- Friend functions
- Operators and friend operators

Basics of Object-Oriented Programming

We live in a world of objects. Each object has its characteristics and operations, and some objects are more animated than others. You can categorize objects into classes. For example, my VW Quantum car is an object that belongs to the class of the VW Quantum model. You can also relate individual classes in a class hierarchy. The class of VW Quantum model is part of the vehicle class hierarchy. Object-oriented programming (OOP) uses the notions of real-world objects to develop applications. The basics of OOP include classes, objects, messages, methods, inheritance, and polymorphism.

Classes and Objects

A class defines a category of objects. Each object is an instance of a class. An object shares the same attributes and functionality with other objects in the same class. Typically, an object has a unique state, defined by the current values of its attributes. The functionality of a class determines the operations that are possible for the class instances. C++ calls the attributes of a class *data members* and calls the operations of a class *member functions*. Classes encapsulate data members and member functions.

Messages and Methods

Object-oriented programming models the interaction with objects as events in which messages are sent to an object or between objects. The object receiving a message responds by invoking the appropriate method (that's the member function in C++). The *message* is *what* is done to an object. The *method* is *how* the object responds to the incoming message. C++ does not explicitly foster the notion of messages and methods as do other OOP languages, such as SmallTalk.

Inheritance

In object-oriented languages, you can derive a class from another class. The derived class (also called the descendant class) inherits the data members and member functions of its parent and ancestor classes. The purpose of deriving a class is to refine the parent class by adding new attributes and new operations. The derived class typically declares new data members and new member functions. In addition, the derived class can also override inherited member functions when the operations of these functions are not suitable for the derived class.

Polymorphism

Polymorphism is an OOP feature that allows the instances of different classes to react in a particular way to a message (or function invocation, in C++ terms). For example, in a hierarchy of graphical shapes (point, line, square, rectangle, circle, ellipse, and so on), each shape has a Draw() function that is responsible for properly responding to a request to draw that shape.

Declaring Base Classes

C++ empowers you to declare a class that encapsulates data members and member functions. These functions alter the values of the data members.

Syntax at a Glance

Declaring a Base Class
The syntax for declaring a base class is

```
class className
{
    private:
            <private data members>
            <private constructors>
            <private member functions>

    protected:
            <protected data members>
            <protected constructors>
            <protected member functions>

    public:
            <public data members>
            <public constructors>
            <public destructor>
            <public member functions>
};
```

Example:

```
class String
{
    protected:
            char* str;     // pointer to characters
            unsigned len;  // current length of
                           // string
            unsigned max;  // max length of string

    public:
            String();            // default
                                 // constructor
```

continues

Declaring a Base Class *continued*

```
        String(String& s); // copy constructor
        ~String();          // destructor

        void assign(String& s);
        unsigned getLen();
        char* getString();
        String& assign(String& s);
        String& concat(String& s1, String& s2);
    };
```

The Sections of a Class

The preceding syntax shows that the declaration involves the keyword class. C++ classes offer three levels of visibility for the various members (that is, both data members and member functions):

■ The private section: only the member functions of the class can access the private members. The class instances are denied access to private members.

■ The protected section: only the member functions of the class and its descendant classes can access protected members. The class instances are denied access to protected members.

■ The public section: this section specifies members that are visible to the member functions of the class, class instances, member functions of descendant classes, and their instances.

Rules for Sections

The following rules apply to the various sections:

■ The class sections can appear in any order.

■ The class sections can appear more than once.

■ If no class section is specified, the C++ compiler treats the members as protected.

■ Avoid placing data members in the public section unless such a declaration significantly simplifies your design. Data members are typically placed in the protected section to allow their access by member functions of descendant classes.

■ Use member functions to set and query the values of data members. The member functions that set the data members assist in performing validation and updating other data members, if need be.

■ The class can have multiple constructors, which are typically located in the public section.

■ The class can have only one destructor, which must be declared in the public section.

■ The member functions (as well as the constructors and destructors) that have multiple statements are defined out-side the class declaration. The definition can reside in the same file that declares the class. In software libraries, the definition of the member functions typically resides in a separate source file. When you define a member function, you must qualify the function name with the class name. The syntax of such a qualification involves using the class name, followed by two colons (::) and then the name of a function. For example, consider the following class:

```
class String
{
    public:
        String();        // default constructor
        ~String();       // destructor

        void assign(String& s);
        // other member functions
};
```

The definitions of the constructor, destructor, and member function are as shown here:

```
String::String()
{
    // sequence of statements
}

String::~String()
{
    // sequence of statements
}

String::assign(String& s)
{
    // sequence of statements
}
```

After you declare a class, you can use the class name as a type identifier to declare class instances. The syntax resembles the syntax used for declaring variables.

Example of a Class

Consider an example of a simple class. Listing 10.1 contains the source code for the LST10_01.CPP program. The listing declares the class Complex to model complex numbers.

Listing 10.1. The source code for the LST10_01.CPP program.

```
// LST10_01.CPP
// simple complex class (version 1)

#include <iostream.h>
#include <conio.h>

class Complex
{
   protected:
     double real;
     double imag;

   public:
     Complex()
        { assign(); }
     void assign(double realVal = 0, double imagVal = 0);
     double getReal()
        { return real; }
     double getImag()
        { return imag; }
     void add(Complex& c1, Complex& c2);
     void print();
};

void Complex::assign(double realVal, double imagVal)
{
  real = realVal;
  imag = imagVal;
}

void Complex::add(Complex& c1, Complex& c2)
{
  real = c1.real + c2.real;
  imag = c2.imag + c2. imag;
}

void Complex::print()
{
  if (real >= 0)
    cout << real << " +i ";
  else
    cout << "(" << real << ") +i ";
  if (imag >= 0)
```

```
    cout << imag;
  else
    cout << "(" << imag << ")";
}

main()
{
  Complex c1, c2, c3;

  c1.assign(2, 3);
  c2.assign(4, -1);
  c3.add(c1, c2);

  clrscr();
  cout << "c1 = ";
  c1.print();
  cout << "\nc2 = ";
  c2.print();
  cout << "\nc1 + c2 = ";
  c3.print();
  cout << "\n\n";

  return 0;
}
```

The class Complex declares two data members, real and imag, that are located in the protected section. These members store the real and imaginary components of a complex number.

The class also declares a constructor (more about constructors in the next section) and a set of member functions. The constructor initializes a class instance by invoking the assign() member function. The class declares the following member functions:

■ The assign() function assigns values to the data members real and imag using the arguments of the parameters realVal and imagVal, respectively. The function has default arguments of 0 for each parameter. The class constructor uses these default arguments to initialize a class instance.

■ The getReal() and getImag() functions return the values of the data members real and imag, respectively. These functions are defined in the class declaration. Each function uses a single statement. The compiler interprets this style of function definition as a request (not an order) to use the function as an inline function.

■ The add() function adds two complex numbers and assigns the result to the targeted class instance.

■ The `print()` function displays the real and imaginary components of a complex number, using `cout`. Negative values of either component are enclosed in parentheses.

The output of Listing 10.1 is shown here:

```
c1 = 2 +i 3
c2 = 4 +i (-1)
c1 + c2 = 6 +i (-2)
```

Constructors

C++ constructors and destructors work automatically to guarantee the appropriate creation and removal of a class instance.

Constructors
The syntax of constructors is

```
class className
{
    public:
        className(); // default constructor
        className(className& c); // copy
                                 // constructor
        className(<parameter list>); // another
                                     // constructor
};
```

Example:

```
class Complex
{
    protected:
        double real;
        double imag;

    public:
        Complex();
        Complex(Complex& c);
        Complex(double realVal,
                double imagVal);
        // other member functions
};
```

Constructor Rules

C++ has the following features and rules regarding constructors:

■ The name of the constructor must be identical to the name of its class.

■ You must not include any return type, not even `void`.

■ A class can have any number of constructors, including none. In the latter case, the compiler automatically creates a constructor for that class.

■ The default constructor is the one that either has no parameters or possesses a parameter list in which all the parameters use default arguments. Here are two examples:

```
// class using a parameterless constructor
class Complex1
{
    protected:
        double real;
        double imag;

    public:
        complex1();
        // other members
};

// class using a constructor with default arguments
class Complex2
{
    protected:
        double real;
        double imag;

    public:
        Complex2(double realVal = 0,
                 double imagVal = 0);
        // other members
};
```

■ The copy constructor enables you to create a class instance using an existing instance. Here is an example:

```
class Complex
{
    protected:
        double real;
```

```
        double imag;

public:
        Complex(); // default constructor
        Complex(Complex& c); // copy constructor
        Complex(double Real, double Imag);
        // other members
};
```

☛ If you do not declare a copy constructor, the compiler creates one. The compiler uses these constructors in creating copies of class instances. Many C++ programmers strongly recommend that you declare copy constructors, especially for classes that model dynamic data structures. These constructors perform what is called a *deep copy,* which includes the dynamic data. By contrast, the compiler creates what is called *shallow copy* constructors, which copy the data members only.

■ The declaration of a class instance (which includes function parameters and local instances) involves a constructor. Which constructor is called? The answer depends on how many constructors you have declared for the class and how you declared the class instance. For example, consider the following instances of the previous version of class Complex:

```
Complex c1; // invokes the default constructor
Complex c2(1.1, 1.3); // uses the third constructor
Complex c3(c2); // uses the copy constructor
```

Because instance c1 specifies no arguments, the compiler uses the default constructor. The c2 instance specifies two floating-point arguments. Consequently, the compiler uses the third constructor. The c3 instance has the c2 instance as an argument. Therefore, the compiler uses the copy constructor to create instance c3 from instance c2.

Destructors

C++ classes can contain destructors that automatically remove class instances.

10

Destructors
The syntax of a destructor is

```
class className
{
    public:
        className(); // default constructor
        // other constructors
        ~className();
        // other member functions
};
```

Example:

```
class String
{
    protected:
        char *str;
        int len;

    public:
        String();
        String(String& s);
        ~String();
        // other member functions
};
```

Destructor Rules

C++ has the following features and rules regarding destructors:

- The name of the destructor must begin with the tilde character (~). The rest of the destructor name must be identical to the name of its class.

- You must not include any return type, not even void.

- A class can have no more than one destructor. If you omit the destructor, the compiler automatically creates one.

- The destructor cannot have any parameters.

- The runtime system automatically invokes a class destructor when the instance of that class is out of scope.

Example of Constructors and Destructors

Consider a program that typifies the use of constructors and
destructors. Listing 10.2 contains the source code for the
LST10_02.CPP program. The program manipulates dynamic arrays
that are modeled by the class Array.

Listing 10.2. The source code for the LST10_02.CPP program.

```
// LST10_02.CPP
// Program demonstrates constructors and destructors

#include <iostream.h>
#include <conio.h>

const unsigned MIN_SIZE = 4;

class Array
{
   protected:
     unsigned *dataPtr;
     unsigned size;

   public:
     Array(unsigned Size = MIN_SIZE);
     Array(Array& ar)
       { copy(ar); }
     ~Array()
       { delete [] dataPtr; }
     unsigned getSize() const
       { return size; }
     void store(unsigned x, unsigned index)
       { dataPtr[index] = x; }
     unsigned recall(unsigned index)
       { return dataPtr[index]; }
     Array& copy(Array& ar);

};

Array::Array(unsigned Size)
{
  size = (Size < MIN_SIZE) ? MIN_SIZE : Size;
  dataPtr = new unsigned[size];
}

Array& Array::copy(Array& ar)
{
  delete [] dataPtr; // delete the current array
  // make size of instance equal to size of argument
  size = ar.size;
  // re-create new array
```

```
    dataPtr = new unsigned[size];
    // copy elements
    for (unsigned i = 0; i < size; i++)
      dataPtr[i] = ar.dataPtr[i];
    return *this;
}

main()
{
  Array Ar1;
  Array Ar2(6);

  for (unsigned i = 0; i < Ar1.getSize(); i++)
    Ar1.store(i * i, i);

  for (i = 0; i < Ar2.getSize(); i++)
    Ar2.store(i + 2, i);

  clrscr();
  cout << "Array Ar1 has the following values:\n\n";
  for (i = 0; i < Ar1.getSize(); i++)
    cout << "Ar1[" << i << "] = " << Ar1.recall(i) << "\n";

  cout << "\n\nPress any key to continue..."; getch();

  clrscr();
  cout << "Array Ar2 has the following values:\n\n";
  for (i = 0; i < Ar2.getSize(); i++)
    cout << "Ar2[" << i << "] = " << Ar2.recall(i) << "\n";

  cout << "\n\nPress any key to continue..."; getch();

  Ar1.copy(Ar2);

  clrscr();
  cout << "Expanded array Ar1 (=Array Ar2)"
       << " has the following values:\n\n";
  for (i = 0; i < Ar1.getSize(); i++)
      cout << "Ar1[" << i << "] = " << Ar1.recall(i) << "\n";
  cout << "\n\nPress any key to end the program..."; getch();

  return 0;

}
```

The class Array declares two data members, two constructors, a
destructor, and four member functions. The data member dataPtr
is the pointer to the elements of the dynamic array. The data member size stores the number of the array elements. I coded the class
such that the array size never goes below a minimum value defined
by the global constant MIN_SIZE.

The class defines two constructors. The first constructor, `Array(unsigned)`, has a single parameter that uses a default argument. This argument allows the compiler to use this constructor as the default constructor. The second constructor is the copy constructor, which merely invokes the `copy()` function to duplicate the elements of one array into the targeted class instance.

The destructor performs the simple, yet necessary, task of removing the dynamically allocated space.

The class `Array` declares the following member functions:

1. The function `getSize()` returns the current size of the array.

2. The function `store()` saves the parameter x at the array index specified by the parameter `index`. To simplify the code, I eliminated range checking for the `index` parameter.

3. The function `recall()` returns the value of the array element at the index specified by the parameter `index`. To simplify the code, I eliminated range checking for the `index` parameter.

4. The `copy()` function duplicates the targeted class instance using the array specified by the parameter ar. Notice that the `copy()` function returns a reference to the class `Array`. In addition, the parameter ar is a reference parameter. Using reference parameters enables you to skip creating a copy of the argument—a step that involves calling the copy constructor of class `Array`. The `copy()` function performs the following tasks:

   ■ Deletes the element of the targeted class instance.

   ■ Assigns the `size` member of the argument to the `size` member of the targeted class instance.

   ■ Creates a new dynamic array whose size matches that of the parameter ar.

   ■ Uses a `for` loop to copy the elements of the array ar into the elements of the targeted class instance.

   ■ Returns the object `*this`.

☛ When you write a member function that returns the reference to the host class, always return `*this`. The identifier `this` points to the targeted class instance, and the expression `*this` returns the targeted instance itself.

The function `main()` manipulates the two instances, Ar1 and Ar2, of class Array. The function creates these instances using the following statements:

```
Array Ar1;
Array Ar2(6);
```

The `main()` function creates instance Ar1 using the first constructor, acting as the default constructor. By contrast, the function builds the instance Ar2 by supplying the first constructor with an explicit size. If you place a breakpoint at any statement in the first constructor and run the program, you will notice that the program execution stops twice at the breakpoint—once for each instance.

The `main()` function assigns values to the instances Ar1 and Ar2 and then displays them. Then the function uses the copy() member function to copy the size and elements of instance Ar2 into instance Ar1. After copying the arrays, the `main()` function displays the elements of the updated instance of Ar1.

Here is the output from the program in Listing 10.2:

```
Array Ar1 has the following values:

Ar1[0] = 0
Ar1[1] = 1
Ar1[2] = 4
Ar1[3] = 9


Press any key to continue...


Array Ar2 has the following values:

Ar2[0] = 2
Ar2[1] = 3
Ar2[2] = 4
Ar2[3] = 5
Ar2[4] = 6
Ar2[5] = 7


Press any key to continue...


Expanded array Ar1 (=Array Ar2) has the following values:

Ar1[0] = 2
Ar1[1] = 3
Ar1[2] = 4
```

```
Ar1[3] = 5
Ar1[4] = 6
Ar1[5] = 7

Press any key to end the program...
```

Static Members

In many applications, you need to use special data members that conceptually belong to the class itself rather than any class instance. Here are a few cases in which such data members are useful:

- Tracking the number of class instances.

- Allocating a special memory block for the various class instances.

- Using arrays of structures to implement a miniature database commonly used by the various class instances.

C++ enables you to use *static* data members for such purposes. You need to observe the following rules:

- Declare the static data member by placing the `static` keyword before the member's data type.

- You can access the static members inside the member functions just like any other nonstatic data members.

- You must initialize the static members outside the class declaration, even if these members are protected or private.

- The static data members exist separately from the class instances. You therefore can access them before you create any class instance.

C++ also enables you to declare static member functions to access the static data members. To declare a static member function, place the `static` keyword before the function's return type. Static member functions *must never* return the expression `*this` and should not access nonstatic data members.

When you access a public static data member or static member function, you need to use the class name as a qualifier.

Example of Static Members

Consider a simple application of static data members. Listing 10.3
shows the source code for the LST10_03.CPP program. This program is based on the preceding one, except it uses static members
to keep track of the number of instances of class Array.

Listing 10.3. The source code for the LST10_03.CPP program.

```
// LST10_03.CPP
// Program demonstrates using static data members to count
// the number of class instances

#include <iostream.h>
#include <conio.h>

const unsigned MIN_SIZE = 4;

class Array
{
   protected:
     unsigned *dataPtr;
     unsigned size;
     static unsigned countInstances;

   public:
     Array(unsigned Size = MIN_SIZE);
     Array(Array& ar);
     ~Array();
     unsigned getSize() const
       { return size; }
     static unsigned getCountInstances()
       { return countInstances; }
     void store(unsigned x, unsigned index)
       { dataPtr[index] = x; }
     unsigned recall(unsigned index)
       { return dataPtr[index]; }
     Array& copy(Array& ar);

};

Array::Array(unsigned Size)
{
  size = (Size < MIN_SIZE) ? MIN_SIZE : Size;
  dataPtr = new unsigned[size];
  countInstances++;
}

Array::Array(Array& ar)
{
  copy(ar);
```

continues

Listing 10.3. Continued

```
  countInstances++;
}

Array::~Array()
{
  delete [] dataPtr;
  countInstances--;
}

Array& Array::copy(Array& ar)
{
  delete [] dataPtr; // delete the current array
  // make size of instance equal to size of argument
  size = ar.size;
  // re-create new array
  dataPtr = new unsigned[size];
  // copy elements
  for (unsigned i = 0; i < size; i++)
    dataPtr[i] = ar.dataPtr[i];
  return *this;
}

// initialize the static member
unsigned Array::countInstances = 0;

main()
{
  Array Ar1;

  for (unsigned i = 0; i < Ar1.getSize(); i++)
    Ar1.store(i * i, i);

  clrscr();
  cout << "Array Ar1 has the following values:\n\n";
  for (i = 0; i < Ar1.getSize(); i++)
      cout << "Ar1[" << i << "] = " << Ar1.recall(i) << "\n";

  cout << "\nThere are " << Array::getCountInstances()
       << " instance(s) of class Array"
       << "\nPress any key to continue...";
  getch();

  {
    Array Ar2(6);

    clrscr();
    for (i = 0; i < Ar2.getSize(); i++)
      Ar2.store(i + 2, i);

    cout << "Array Ar2 has the following values:\n\n";
    for (i = 0; i < Ar2.getSize(); i++)
      cout << "Ar2[" << i << "] = " << Ar2.recall(i) << "\n";
```

```
    cout << "\nThere are " << Array::getCountInstances()
         << " instance(s) of class Array"
         << "\nPress any key to continue...";
    getch();
    // copy elements of array Ar1 to array Ar1
    Ar1.copy(Ar2);
  }

  clrscr();
  cout << "Expanded array Ar1 (=Array Ar2)"
       << " has the following values:\n\n";
  for (i = 0; i < Ar1.getSize(); i++)
    cout << "Ar1[" << i << "] = " << Ar1.recall(i) << "\n";
  cout << "\nThere are " << Array::getCountInstances()
       << " instance(s) of class Array"
       << "\nPress any key to continue...";
  getch();

  return 0;

}
```

The new version of class Array declares the static countInstances
member to keep track of the number of class instances. Notice that
the program initializes the static data member outside the class
declaration using the following statement:

```
unsigned Array::countInstances = 0;
```

In addition, notice that the constructors increment the member
countInstances. By contrast, the destructor decrements this static
data member. These actions enable the class to keep track of the
current number of instances as client functions create and destroy
them.

The class also declares the static member function
getCountInstances() to return the value stored in the
countInstances member. The various member functions
access the member countInstances just like the other two nonstatic data members.

I modified the main() function to declare the Ar2 instance in a
nested block. This declaration enables the Ar2 instance to be created later in the main() function and to be removed before the end
of the function. When the main() function displays the elements of
instances Ar1 or Ar2, it also includes the current number of class
instances. main() displays this information by calling the static
function getCountInstances(). Notice that this function requires
the code to qualify countInstances by using the class name, Array.

Here is the output of the program in Listing 10.3:

```
Array Ar1 has the following values:

Ar1[0] = 0
Ar1[1] = 1
Ar1[2] = 4
Ar1[3] = 9

There are 1 instance(s) of class Array
Press any key to continue...

Array Ar2 has the following values:

Ar2[0] = 2
Ar2[1] = 3
Ar2[2] = 4
Ar2[3] = 5
Ar2[4] = 6
Ar2[5] = 7

There are 2 instance(s) of class Array
Press any key to continue...

Expanded array Ar1 (=Array Ar2) has the following values:

Ar1[0] = 2
Ar1[1] = 3
Ar1[2] = 4
Ar1[3] = 5
Ar1[4] = 6
Ar1[5] = 7

There are 1 instance(s) of class Array
Press any key to continue...
```

Friend Functions

C++ allows member functions to access all the data members of a
class. In addition, C++ grants the same privileged access to *friend*
functions. Friend functions are ordinary functions that have access
to all data members of one or more classes. The declaration of
friend functions appears in the class and begins with the keyword
friend. Other than using the special keyword, friend functions
look very much like member functions (except they cannot return
a reference to the befriended class, because such result requires
returning the self-reference *this). However, when you define
friend functions outside the declaration of their befriended class,
you need not qualify the function names with the name of
the class.

Friend Functions

The general form of a friend function is

```
class className
{
    public:
        className();
        // other constructors

        friend returnType
            friendFunction(<parameter list>);
};
```

Example:

```
class String
{
    protected:
        char *str;
        int len;

    public:
        String();
        ~String();
        // other member functions
        friend String& concat(String& s1,
                                String& s2);
        friend String& concat(const char* s1,
                                String& s2);
        friend String& concat(String& s1,
                                const char* s2);
};
main()
{
  String s1, s2, s3;
  s1 = "Hello ";
  s2 = concat(s1, "World!")
  s3 = concat("He said: ", s2);
  cout << s3 << "\n";
  return 0;
}
```

10

Friend classes can accomplish tasks that are awkward, difficult, and even impossible with member functions.

Example of Friend Functions

Consider a simple example of using friend functions. Listing 10.4 contains the source code for the LST10_04.CPP program. This program performs very simple manipulation of complex numbers.

Listing 10.4. The source code for the LST10_04.CPP program.

```
// LST10_04.CPP
// Program demonstrates friend functions

#include <iostream.h>
#include <conio.h>

class Complex
{
    protected:
      double real;
      double imag;

    public:
      Complex(double realVal = 0, double imagVal = 0);
      Complex(Complex& c)
        { assign(c); }
      void assign(Complex& c);
      double getReal() const
        { return real; }
      double getImag() const
        { return imag; }
      friend Complex add(Complex& c1, Complex& c2);
};

Complex::Complex(double realVal, double imagVal)
{
  real = realVal;
  imag = imagVal;
}

void Complex::assign(Complex& c)
{
  real = c.real;
  imag = c.imag;
}

Complex add(Complex& c1, Complex& c2)
{
  Complex result(c1);
```

```
  result.real += c2.real;
  result.imag += c2.imag;
  return result;
}

main()
{
  Complex c1(1, 1);
  Complex c2(2, 2);
  Complex c3;

  clrscr();
  c3.assign(add(c1, c2));

  cout << "(" << c1.getReal() << " + i" << c1.getImag() << ")"
       << " + "
       << "(" << c2.getReal() << " + i" << c2.getImag() << ")"
       << " = "
       << "(" << c3.getReal() << " + i" << c3.getImag() << ")"
       << "\n\n";

  getch();
  return 0;
}
```

The class Complex, which models complex numbers, declares two data members, two constructors, a friend function (the highlight of this example), and a set of member functions. The data members real and imag store the real and imaginary components of a complex number.

The class has two constructors. The first constructor has two parameters (with default arguments) that enable you to build a class instance using the real and imaginary components of a complex number. Because the two parameters have default arguments, the constructor doubles as the default constructor. The second constructor, Complex(Complex&), is the copy constructor that enables you to create class instances by copying the data from existing instances.

The complex class declares three member functions. The function assign() copies a class instance into another class instance. The functions getReal() and getImag() return the value stored in the members real and imag, respectively.

☛ The Complex class declares the friend function add() to add two complex numbers. To make the program short, I did not implement complementary friend functions that subtract, multiply, and divide class instances. What is so special about the friend function add()? Why not use an ordinary member function to add a class instance? To answer the question, I'll present the declaration of the alternative add() member function:

```
Complex& add(Complex& c)
```

This declaration states that the function treats the parameter c as a second operand. Here is how the alternative member function add() would work:

```
Complex c1(3, 4), c2(1.2, 4.5);
c1.add(c2); // adds c2 to c1
```

First, the member function add() works as an increment and not as an addition function. Second, the targeted class instance is always the first operand. Although this is not a problem for operations such as addition and multiplication, it is a problem for subtraction and division. That is why the friend function add() works better, by giving you the freedom of choosing how to add the class instances. In addition, you can write overloaded versions of function add() in which the first parameter is not the type Complex. This flexibility gives friend functions an advantage over member functions in providing more flexible ways to write expressions.

The friend function add() returns a class instance. The function creates a local instance of class Complex and returns that instance.

The main() function uses the member function assign() and the friend function add() to perform simple complex operations. In addition, the main() function invokes the functions getReal() and getImag() with the various instances of class Complex to display the components of each instance.

Operators and Friend Operators

The program in Listing 10.4 uses a member function and a friend function to implement complex math operations. This approach is typical in C and Pascal, because these languages do not support user-defined operators. By contrast, C++ enables you to declare operators and friend operators. These operators include +, -, *, /, %, ==, !=, <=, <, >=, >, +=, -=, *=, /=, %=, [], (), <<, and >>. See the various operator tables in Chapter 3, "Variables and Operators," to refresh yourself on the use of these operators. C++ treats operators and friend operators as special member functions and friend functions.

Declaring Operators and Friend Operators
The syntax for declaring operators and friend operators is

```
class className
{
    public:
        // constructors and destructor
        // member functions

        // unary operator
        returnType operator
            operatorSymbol(operand);
        // binary operator
        returnType operator
            operatorSymbol(firstOperand,
                           secondOperand);
        // unary friend operator
        friend returnType
            operator operatorSymbol(operand);
        // binary operator
        friend returnType operator
            operatorSymbol(firstOperand,
                           secondOperand);
};
```

Example:

```
class String

{
    protected:
        char *str;
        int len;

    public:
        String();
        ~String();
        // other member functions
        // assignment operator
        String& operator =(String& s);
        String& operator +=(String& s);
        // concatenation operators
```

continuos

Declaring Operators and Friend Operators
continued

```
        friend String& operator +(String& s1,
                                   String& s2);
        friend String& operator +(const char* s1,
                                   String& s2);
        friend String& operator +(String& s1,
                                   const char* s2);
        // relational operators
        friend int operator >(String& s1,
                              String& s2);
        friend int operator =>(String& s1,
                              String& s2);
        friend int operator <(String& s1,
                              String& s2);
        friend int operator <=(String& s1,
                              String& s2);
        friend int operator ==(String& s1,
                              String& s2);
        friend int operator !=(String& s1,
                              String& s2);
};
```

The client functions use the operators and friend operators just like predefined operators. Therefore, you can create operators to support the operations of classes that model, for example, complex numbers, strings, arrays, and matrices. These operators enable you to write expressions that are far more readable than expressions that use named functions.

Example of Operators and Friend Functions

Consider an example. Listing 10.5 contains the source code for the LST10_05.CPP program. This program is a modification of Listing 10.4.

Listing 10.5. The source code for the LST10_05.CPP program.

```
// LST10_05.CPP
// Program demonstrates operators and friend operators

#include <iostream.h>
#include <conio.h>
```

```
class Complex
{
   protected:
     double real;
     double imag;

   public:
     Complex(double Real = 0, double Imag = 0)
       { assign(Real, Imag); }
     Complex(Complex& c);
     void assign(double Real = 0, double Imag = 0);
     double getReal() const
       { return real; }
     double getImag() const
       { return imag; }
     Complex& operator =(Complex& c);
     Complex& operator +=(Complex& c);
     friend Complex operator +(Complex& c1, Complex& c2);
     friend ostream& operator <<(ostream& os, Complex& c);
};

Complex::Complex(Complex& c)
{
  real = c.real;
  imag = c.imag;
}

void Complex::assign(double Real, double Imag)
{
  real = Real;
  imag = Imag;
}

Complex& Complex::operator =(Complex& c)
{
  real = c.real;
  imag = c.imag;
  return *this;
}

Complex& Complex::operator +=(Complex& c)
{
  real += c.real;
  imag += c.imag;
  return *this;
}

Complex operator +(Complex& c1, Complex& c2)
{
  Complex result(c1);

  result.real += c2.real;
  result.imag += c2.imag;
```

continues

Listing 10.5. Continued

```
  return result;
}

ostream& operator <<(ostream& os, Complex& c)
{
  os << "(" << c.real
     << " + i" << c.imag << ")";

  return os;
}

main()
{
  Complex c1(1, 1);
  Complex c2(2, 2);
  Complex c3;
  Complex c4(4, 4);

  clrscr();
  c3 = c1 + c2;
  cout << c1 << " + " << c2 << " = " << c3 << "\n\n";
  cout << c3 << " + " << c4 << " = ";
  c3 += c4;
  cout << c3 << "\n\n";
  getch();
  return 0;
}
```

The new class Complex replaces the assign(Complex&) member function with the operator =. The class also replaces the friend function add() with the friend operator +:

```
Complex& operator =(Complex& c);
friend Complex operator +(Complex& c1, Complex& c2);
```

The operator = has one parameter, a reference to an instance of class Complex, and it returns a reference to the same class. The friend operator + has two parameters (both are references to instances of class Complex) and yields a complex class type.

I also took the opportunity to add two new operators:

```
complex& operator +=(complex& c);
friend ostream& operator <<(ostream& os, complex& c);
```

☞ The operator += is a member of class Complex. This operator takes one parameter, a reference to an instance of class Complex, and yields a reference to the same class. The other new operator is the friend operator <<, which illustrates how to write a stream extractor operator for a class. The friend operator has two parameters: a reference to class `ostream` (the output stream class) and a reference to class `Complex`. The operator `<<` returns a reference to class `ostream`. This type of value enables you to chain stream output with other predefined types or other classes (assuming that these classes have a friend operator `<<`). The definition of friend operator `<<` has two statements. The first statement outputs strings and the data members of class `Complex` to the output stream parameter `os`. The friendship status of operator `<<` allows it to access the `real` and `imag` data members of its `Complex`-typed parameter `c`. The second statement in the operator definition returns the first parameter `os`.

The `main()` function declares four instances of class `Complex`: `c1`, `c2`, `c3`, and `c4`. The instances `c1`, `c2`, and `c4` are created with nondefault values assigned to the data members `real` and `imag`. The function tests using the operators `=`, `+`, `<<`, `+=`. The program illustrates that using operators and friend operators, you can write code that is more readable and supports a higher level of abstraction.

Here is the output of the program in Listing 10.5:

```
(1 + i1) + (2 + i2) = (3 + i3)

(3 + i3) + (4 + i4) = (7 + i7)
```

☛ Following is another example to illustrate a special use of the operator `[]`. Listing 10.6 contains the source code for the LST10_06.CPP program. This program uses a dynamic array to calculate, store, and display Fibonacci numbers. These numbers are generated by the following simple sequence of numbers:

```
Fibonacci(0) = 0
Fibonacci(1) = 1
Fibonacci(i) = Fibonacci(i-1) + Fibonacci(i-2)
```

Listing 10.6. The source code for the LST10_06.CPP program.

```cpp
// LST10_06.CPP
// Program demonstrates using the operator []

#include <iostream.h>
#include <conio.h>

const unsigned MIN_SIZE = 10;
const double BAD_VALUE = -1.0e+30;

class Array
{
   protected:
```

continues

Listing 10.6. Continued

```
    double *dataPtr;
    unsigned size;
    double badIndex;

  public:
    Array(unsigned Size = MIN_SIZE);
    ~Array()
      { delete [] dataPtr; }
    unsigned getSize() const
      { return size; }
    double& operator [](unsigned index);
};

Array::Array(unsigned Size)
{
  size = (Size < MIN_SIZE) ? MIN_SIZE : Size;
  badIndex = BAD_VALUE;
  dataPtr = new double[size];
}

double& Array::operator [](unsigned index)
{
  if (index < size)
    return *(dataPtr + index);
  else
    return badIndex;
}

main()
{
  Array fibonacci(15);

  clrscr();
  fibonacci[0] = 0;
  fibonacci[1] = 1;
  for (unsigned i = 2; i < fibonacci.getSize(); i++)
    fibonacci[i] = fibonacci[i-1] + fibonacci[i - 2];

  for (i = 0; i < fibonacci.getSize() + 2; i++)
    cout << "Fibonacci(" << i << ") = " << fibonacci[i]
         << "\n";
  getch();
  return 0;
}
```

The class Array models a dynamic array of floating-point numbers with minimal functionality. The class declares three data members: dataPtr, size, and badIndex. The dataPtr member is a pointer used to access the dynamic array of doubles. The member size stores the number of elements in a class instance. The `badIndex` member provides a value for out-of-range indices.

The highlight of the class `Array` is the operator `[]`. This operator has one parameter that passes the arguments for the array indices. The operator returns a reference to the type `double`. If the value of the parameter `index` is within the valid range, the operator returns a reference to the sought array element. Otherwise, the operator yields the reference to the data member `badIndex`.

The versatility of the operator `[]` comes from the fact that it returns a reference type. Such a return type enables the operator to be used on both sides of an assignment operator. This is exactly what you see in the first `for` loop located in the `main()` function. Notice that `main()` accesses each element of array `fibonacci` using the operator `[]` as though it were an array of a predefined data type! Thus, using the `[]` operator enables you to support a level of abstraction for class-based arrays that is similar to the abstraction offered for arrays of predefined types.

Here is the output of the program in Listing 10.6:

```
Fibonacci(0) = 0
Fibonacci(1) = 1
Fibonacci(2) = 1
Fibonacci(3) = 2
Fibonacci(4) = 3
Fibonacci(5) = 5
Fibonacci(6) = 8
Fibonacci(7) = 13
Fibonacci(8) = 21
Fibonacci(9) = 34
Fibonacci(10) = 55
Fibonacci(11) = 89
Fibonacci(12) = 144
Fibonacci(13) = 233
Fibonacci(14) = 377
Fibonacci(15) = -1e+30
Fibonacci(16) = -1e+30
```

Summary

This chapter introduced C++ classes and discussed the following topics:

■ Basics of object-oriented programming. These include classes, objects, messages, methods, inheritance, and polymorphism.

■ Declaring base classes to specify the various private, protected, and public members. C++ classes contain data members and member functions. The data members store the state of a class instance, and the member functions query and manipulate that state.

■ Constructors and destructors support the automatic creation and removal of class instances. Constructors are special members that must have the same name as the host class. You can declare any number of constructors, or none. In the latter case, the compiler creates a constructor for you. Each constructor enables you to create a class instance in a different way. There are two special kinds of constructors: the default constructor and the copy constructor. C++ enables you to declare only one parameterless destructor, in contrast with constructors. The runtime system automatically invokes the constructor and destructor when a class instance comes into and goes out of its scope.

■ Static members are special members that conceptually belong to the class itself rather than any particular instance. C++ supports static data members and member functions. There is only one copy of a static data member, regardless of how many class instances exist. Static data members enable you to store data that is relevant to the class itself, such as the number of instances or an information table commonly used by all the class instances.

■ Friend functions are special nonmember functions that can access protected and private data members. These functions enable you to implement operations that are more flexible than those offered by member functions.

■ Operators and friend operators enable you to support various operations, such as addition, assignment, and indexing. These operators empower you to offer a level of abstraction for your classes. In addition, they assist in making the expressions that manipulate class instances more readable and more intuitive.

■ Friend classes have the privilege of accessing all the data members of a befriended class. Such a relation enables the friend class to quickly and flexibly alter instances of the befriended classes. Such instances are typically parameters that appear in the member functions of the befriended class.

Advanced Object-Oriented Programming

This chapter looks at more advanced topics in class and hierarchy designs. It covers the following topics:

- Declaring a class hierarchy
- Virtual member functions
- Abstract classes
- Overloading member functions and operators
- Nested data types
- Friend classes
- Multiple inheritance

Declaring a Class Hierarchy

The power of the OOP features of C++ comes from the capability to derive classes from existing ones. A descendant class inherits the members of its ancestor classes (that is, parent class, grandparent class, and so on) and can also override some of the inherited functions. Inheritance empowers you to reuse code in descendant classes.

Declaring a Derived Class

The syntax for declaring a derived class is

```
class className : [public] parentClass
{
        <friend classes>

        private:
                <private data members>
                <private constructors>
                <private member functions>

        protected:
                <protected data members>
                <protected constructors>
                <protected member functions>

        public:
                <public data members>
                <public constructors>
                <public destructor>
                <public member functions>

                <friend functions and/or
                 friend operators>
};
```

Example:

The following example shows the class TCircle and its descendant class, TCylinder.

```
class TCircle
{
        protected:
                double radius;

        public:
                TCircle(double radiusVal);
                double getRadius() const;
                double setRadius(double radiusVal);
                double calcArea();
};
```

```
class TCylinder : public TCircle
{
    protected:
        double height;

    public:
        TCylinder(double radiusVal,
                double heightVal);
        double getHeight() const;
        double setHeight(double heightVal);
        double calcArea();
};
```

The class lineage is indicated by a colon followed by the optional keyword public and then the name of the parent class. When you include the keyword public, you allow the instances of the descendant class to access the public members of the parent and other ancestor classes. By contrast, when you omit the keyword public, you deprive the instance of the descendant class from accessing the members of the ancestor classes.

☛ The data hiding feature is justified when a change in context is brought by the descendant class. For example, consider a class that implements a dynamic list of unsigned integers:

```
class intList
{
    protected:
        unsigned* head;
        unsigned listSize;
        // other members

    public:
        intList();  // constructor
        ~intList(); // destructor
        int insert(unsigned n);
        int search(unsigned n);
        int remove(unsigned n);
        void clearList();
        // other member functions
};
```

Now you can use the preceding class to implement a class that models a list-based stack of unsigned integers:

```
class intStack : intList
{
    public:
```

```
                    intStack(); // constructor
                    ~intStack(); // destructor
                    void push(unsigned n);
                    int pop(unsigned& n);
                    void clearStack();
          };
```

The class intStack is a descendant of class intList. However, you do not want the instances of class intStack to access the public member functions insert(), search(), and remove() because they support operations for lists, not stacks. By omitting the public class derivation, you force the instances of class intStack to use the member functions push(), pop(), and clearStack(). This example shows how the descendant class has changed context while still making use of the operations supported by the parent class.

A descendant class inherits the data members of its ancestor class or classes. C++ has no mechanism for removing unwanted inherited data members—you are basically stuck with them. By contrast, C++ enables you to override inherited member functions. You'll read more about this topic later in this chapter. The descendant class declares new data members, new member functions, and overriding member functions. Again, you can place these members in the private, protected, or public sections as you see fit in your class design.

Example for Deriving Classes

Consider an example that declares a small class hierarchy. Listing 11.1 shows the source code for the LST11_01.CPP program. This program declares classes that contain a hierarchy of simple geometric shapes: a circle, a sphere, a cylinder, and a hollow cylinder.

Listing 11.1. The source code for the LST11_01.CPP program.

```
// LST11_01.CPP
// Program demonstrates a small hierarchy of classes

#include <iostream.h>
#include <conio.h>
#include <math.h>

const double pi = 4 * atan(1);

inline double sqr(double x)
{ return x * x; }
```

```
class TCircle
{
  protected:
    double radius;

  public:
    TCircle(double radiusVal = 0) : radius(radiusVal) {}
    void setRadius(double radiusVal)
      { radius = radiusVal; }
    double getRadius() const
      { return radius; }
    double area() const
      { return pi * sqr(radius); }
    void showData();
};

class TCylinder : public TCircle
{
  protected:
    double height;

  public:
    TCylinder(double heightVal = 0, double radiusVal = 0)
      : height(heightVal), TCircle(radiusVal) {}
    void setHeight(double heightVal)
      { height = heightVal; }
    double getHeight() const
      { return height; }
    double area() const
      { return 2 * TCircle::area() +
              2 * pi * radius * height; }
    void showData();
};

void TCircle::showData()
{
   cout << "Circle radius       = " << getRadius() << "\n"
        << "Circle area         = " << area() << "\n\n";
}

void TCylinder::showData()
{
   cout << "Cylinder radius     = " << getRadius() << "\n"
        << "Cylinder height     = " << getHeight() << "\n"
        << "Cylinder area       = " << area() << "\n\n";
}

main()
{
   TCircle Circle(1);
   TCylinder Cylinder(10, 1);

   clrscr();
   Circle.showData();
```

continues

Listing 11.1. Continued

```
    Cylinder.showData();
    cout << "Press any key to end the program...";
    getch();
    return 0;
}
```

This listing declares the classes TCircle and TCylinder. The class TCircle models a circle, whereas class TCylinder models a cylinder.

The TCircle class declares a single data member, radius, to store the radius of the circle. The class also declares a constructor and a set of member functions. The constructor assigns a value to the data member radius when you declare a class instance. Notice that the constructor uses a new syntax to initialize the member radius. The functions setRadius() and getRadius() set and query the value in member radius, respectively. The function area() returns the area of the circle. The function showData() displays the radius and area of a class instance.

The class TCylinder, a descendant of TCircle, declares a single data member, height, to store the height of the cylinder. The class inherits the member radius needed to store the radius of the cylinder. The TCylinder class declares a constructor and a set of member functions. The constructor assigns values to the radius and height members when creating a class instance. Notice the use of a new syntax to initialize the members—the member height is initialized, and the member radius is initialized by invoking the constructor of class TCircle with the argument radiusVal. The functions setHeight() and getHeight() set and query the value in member height, respectively. The class uses the inherited functions setRadius() and getRadius() to manipulate the inherited member radius. The function area(), which overrides the inherited function TCircle::area(), returns the surface area of the cylinder. Notice that this function explicitly invokes the inherited function TCircle::area(). The function showData() displays the radius, height, and area of a class instance.

The main() function performs the following tasks:

1. Declares the instance Circle, of class TCircle, and assigns 1 to the circle's radius.

2. Declares the instance Cylinder, of class TCylinder, and assigns 10 to the circle's height and 1 to the circle's radius.

3. Invokes the showData() routine for each class instance.

Here is the output for the program in Listing 11.1:

```
Circle radius      = 1
Circle area        = 3.141593

Cylinder radius    = 1
Cylinder height    = 10
Cylinder area      = 69.115038

Press any key to end the program...
```

Virtual Functions

Polymorphic behavior is an important object-oriented programming feature. This feature empowers the instances of different classes to respond to the same function in ways that are appropriate to each class. Consider the following simple classes and the main() function:

```cpp
#include <iostream.h>
class TA
{
    public:
        double A(double x)
            { return x * x; }
        double B(double x)
            { return A(x) / 2; }
};

class TB : public TA
{
    public:
        double A(double x)
            { return x * x * x; }
};

main()
{
    TB aB;
    cout << aB.B(3) << "\n";
    return 0;
}
```

Class TA contains functions A() and B(), where function B() calls function A(). Class TB, a descendant of class TA, inherits function B() but overrides function A(). The intent here is to have the inherited function TA::B() call function TB::A(), in order to support polymorphic behavior. What is the program output? The answer is 4.5 and *not* 13.5! Why? The answer lies in the fact that the compiler resolves the expression aB.B(3) by using the inherited function TA::B(), which in turn calls function TA::A(). Therefore, function TB:A() is left out, and the program fails to support polymorphic behavior.

C++ supports polymorphic behavior by offering *virtual* functions. These functions, which are bound at runtime, are declared by placing the keyword virtual before the function's return type. After you declare a function virtual, you can override it only with virtual functions in descendant classes. These overriding functions *must have* the same parameter list. Virtual functions can override nonvirtual functions in ancestor classes.

Declaring Virtual Functions

The syntax for declaring virtual functions is

```
class className1
{
    // member functions
    virtual returnType
        functionName(<parameter list>);
};

class className2 : public className1
{
    // member functions
    virtual returnType
        functionName(<parameter list>);
};
```

Example:

The following example shows how virtual functions can successfully implement polymorphic behavior in classes TA and TB.

```
#include <iostream.h>
class TA
{
    public:
        virtual double A(double x)
            { return x * x; }
        double B(double x)
            {return A(x) / 2; }
};
```

```
class TB : public TA
{
    public:
        virtual double A(double x)
            { return x * x * x; }
};

main()
{
    TB aB;
    cout << aB.B(3) << "\n";
    return 0;
}
```

This example displays 13.5, the correct result, because the call to the inherited function `TA::B()` is resolved at runtime by calling `TB::A()`.

☛ When do you use virtual functions? When you have a callable function that implements a behavior specific to a class. Declaring such a function as virtual ensures that it provides the correct response that is relevant to the associated class.

Example of Using Virtual Functions

Consider an example. Listing 11.2 shows the source code for the program LST11_02.CPP. The program expands the class hierarchy found in Listing 11.1. The new version has three classes, TCircle, TCylinder, and THollowCylinder. The THollowCylinder class models a hollow cylinder and is a descendant of class TCylinder. The program calculates and displays the area of the circle as well as both the base area and the volume of the two cylinder types.

Listing 11.2. The source code for the LST11_02.CPP program.

```
// LST11_02.CPP
// Program demonstrates virtual functions

#include <iostream.h>
#include <conio.h>
```

continues

Listing 11.2. Continued

```
#include <math.h>

const double pi = 4 * atan(1);

inline double sqr(double x)
{ return x * x; }

class TCircle
{
  protected:
    double radius;

  public:
    TCircle(double radiusVal = 0) : radius(radiusVal) {}
    void setRadius(double radiusVal)
      { radius = radiusVal; }
    double getRadius() const
      { return radius; }
    virtual double area() const
      { return pi * sqr(radius); }
    void showData();
};

class TCylinder : public TCircle
{
  protected:
    double height;

  public:
    TCylinder(double heightVal = 0, double radiusVal = 0)
      : height(heightVal), TCircle(radiusVal) {}
    void setHeight(double heightVal)
      { height = heightVal; }
    double getHeight() const
      { return height; }
    double volume()
      { return height * area(); }
    void showData();
};

class THollowCylinder : public TCylinder
{
  protected:
    double innerRadius;

  public:
    THollowCylinder(double heightVal = 0, double Rin = 0,
                    double Rout = 0) : innerRadius(Rin),
      TCylinder(heightVal, Rout) {}
    void setInnerRadius(double Rin)
      { innerRadius = Rin; }
    double getInnerRadius() const
```

```
         { return innerRadius; }
      virtual double area() const
         { return pi * (sqr(radius) - sqr(innerRadius)); }
      void showData();
};

void TCircle::showData()
{
   cout << "Circle radius      = " << getRadius() << "\n"
        << "Circle area        = " << area() << "\n\n";
}

void TCylinder::showData()
{
   cout << "Cylinder radius    = " << getRadius() << "\n"
        << "Cylinder height    = " << getHeight() << "\n"
        << "Cylinder base area = " << area() << "\n"
        << "Cylinder volume    = " << volume()  << "\n\n";
}

void THollowCylinder::showData()
{
   cout << "Hollow radius       = " << getRadius() << "\n"
        << "Hollow inner radius = " << getInnerRadius()
                                    << "\n"
        << "Hollow height       = " << getHeight() << "\n"
        << "Cylinder base area  = " << area() << "\n"
        << "Hollow volume       = " << volume() << "\n\n";
}

main()
{
   TCircle Circle(1);
   TCylinder Cylinder(10, 1);
   THollowCylinder Hollow(10, 0.5, 1);

   clrscr();
   Circle.showData();
   Cylinder.showData();
   Hollow.showData();
   cout << "\nPress any key to end the program...";
   getch();
   return 0;
}
```

The highlight of Listing 11.2 is the virtual function area() and the function volume(). The volume of the full cylinder is the product of the height and the base area (which is equal to the area of the circular base). The volume of the hollow cylinder is the product of the height and the base area (which is equal to the net area of the circular base).

The class TCircle declares the virtual function area(). Class TCylinder simply inherits the virtual function, because the values returned by TCircle::area() are adequate for class TCylinder. By contrast, class THollowCylinder declares its own virtual function area() to calculate the base area differently.

Class TCylinder declares the function volume() to calculate the volume of a cylinder. This function uses the inherited virtual function TCircle::area(). Interestingly, class THollowCylinder inherits function TCylinder::volume(). This inherited function performs the correct calculation by calling the virtual function THollowCylinder::area().

Here is the output of the program in Listing 11.2:

```
Circle radius       = 1
Circle area         = 3.141593

Cylinder radius     = 1
Cylinder height     = 10
Cylinder base area  = 3.141593
Cylinder volume     = 31.415927

Hollow radius       = 1
Hollow inner radius = 0.5
Hollow height       = 10
Cylinder base area  = 2.356194
Hollow volume       = 23.561945


Press any key to end the program...
```

☞ C++ programmers highly recommend that you declare the destructor as virtual. This ensures polymorphic behavior in destroying class instances.

Abstract Classes

C++ expands the notion of refining classes by derivation through abstract classes. Such classes include the base class of a hierarchy and possibly the first few descendants. The class hierarchy designer can use virtual functions and a special syntax in the abstract classes to influence the evolution of the class hierarchy. The influence over descendant classes occurs through the virtual functions. Remember that when you override an inherited virtual function, you must use the same parameter list.

Abstract Classes

The syntax of an abstract class is

```
class abstractClass
{
    <private members>

    protected:
        // protected data members
        virtual returnType
            function1(<parameter list 1>) = 0;
        virtual returnType
            function2(<parameter list 2>) = 0;
        // other member functions

    public:
        // public data members
        virtual returnType
            function3(<parameter list 3>) = 0;
        virtual returnType
            function4(<parameter list 4>) = 0;
        // other member functions
};
```

Example:

The following class declaration models an abstract array that stores floating-point numbers. The functions `store()`, `recall()`, `swap()`, and `reverse()` are declared as abstract functions. The other member functions have implementations (not included in the book) that use the `store()`, `recall()`, and `swap()` functions to sort and search for array elements.

```
class AbstractArray
{
    protected:
        unsigned workSize;
        unsigned maxSize;

    public:
        virtual boolean store(double x,
                              unsigned index) = 0;
```

continues

> **Abstract Classes *continued***
> ```
>             virtual boolean recall(double& x,
>                                    unsigned index) = 0;
>
>             virtual void swap(index i,
>                               index j) = 0;
>             virtual void reverse() = 0;
>             void quickSort();
>             unsigned linearSearch(double key,
>                                   unsigned start);
>             unsigned binarySearch(double key);
>   };
> ```

To give you a better feel for using abstract classes, examine the following class declarations based on the class `AbstractArray` that appears in the preceding syntax box:

```
class memArray : public AbstractArray
{
      protected:
           double* dataPtr; // pointer to dynamic array

      public:
           memArray(unsigned arraySize);
           ~memArray();
           virtual boolean store(double x, unsigned index);
           virtual boolean recall(double& x, unsigned index);
           virtual void swap(index i, index j);
           virtual void reverse();
};

class VmArray : public AbstractArray
{
      protected:
           fstream f; // C++ file stream

      public:
           VmArray(const char* filename, unsigned arraySize);
           ~VmArray();
           virtual boolean store(double x, unsigned index);
           virtual boolean recall(double& x, unsigned index);
           virtual void swap(index i, index j);
           virtual void reverse();
};
```

The class `memArray` implements a heap-based dynamic array, accessed using the pointer `dataPtr`. The class inherits the `quickSort()`, `linearSearch()`, and `binarySearch()` functions.

By contrast, the class declares its own version of the virtual functions `store()`, `recall()`, `swap()`, and `reverse()`. These functions use the `dataPtr` member to access the elements of the dynamic array in the heap.

The class `VmArray` implements a disk-based virtual dynamic array. This array uses the stream `f` to access the individual array elements in a data file. This class also inherits the `quickSort()`, `linearSearch()`, and `binarySearch()` functions. Like class `memArray`, this class declares its own version of the virtual functions. These functions use the stream `f` to access the elements of the dynamic array.

Overloading Member Functions and Operators

C++ enables you to overload member functions, operators, friend functions, and friend operators. The rules for overloading these functions and operators are the same, within a class, as for overloading ordinary functions.

Example of Overloaded Functions

Listing 11.3 shows a simple example of overloading functions and operators, applied to the class `Complex`. The class overloads the function `assign()`, the operator =, and the friend operator +. Overloading these functions and operators empowers you to write abstract expressions and statements. The overloaded assignment statements enable you to assign the individual components of a complex number, or use an existing class instance. The overloaded = operator enables you to assign a class instance to another, or assign the real number to a class instance. The overloaded friend operator (+) enables you to add two class instances, or add a real number to a class instance. The latter case requires two versions of the operator + to ensure that you cover having either added entity as the first or second operand.

Listing 11.3. The source code for the LST11_03.CPP program.

```
// LST11 03.CPP
// Program that illustrates overloading functions
// and operators
```

continues

Listing 11.3. continued

```cpp
#include <iostream.h>
#include <conio.h>

class Complex
{
   protected:
     double real;
     double imag;

   public:
     Complex()
       { assign(); }
     void assign(double realVal = 0, double imagVal = 0);
     void assign(Complex& c)
       { assign(c.real, c.imag); }
     double getReal()
       { return real; }
     double getImag()
       { return imag; }
     void print();
     Complex& operator =(double realVal)
       { assign(realVal, 0); return *this; }
     Complex& operator =(Complex& c)
       { assign(c); return *this; }
     friend Complex operator+(Complex& c1, Complex& c2);
     friend Complex operator+(Complex& c, double x);
     friend Complex operator+(double x, Complex& c);
};

void Complex::assign(double realVal, double imagVal)
{
  real = realVal;
  imag = imagVal;
}

void Complex::print()
{
  if (real >= 0)
    cout << real << " +i ";
  else
    cout << "(" << real << ") +i ";
  if (imag >= 0)
    cout << imag;
  else
    cout << "(" << imag << ")";
}

Complex operator+(Complex& c1, Complex& c2)
{
  Complex cc(c1);
  cc.real += c2.real;
  cc.imag += c2.imag;
  return cc;
}
```

```
Complex operator+(Complex& c, double x)
{
  Complex cc(c);
  cc.real += x;
  return cc;
}

Complex operator+(double x, Complex& c)
{
  Complex cc(c);
  cc.real += x;
  return cc;
}

main()
{
  Complex c1, c2, c3;

  c1.assign(2, 3);
  c2.assign(4, -1);
  c3 = 2.0 + c1 + c2 + 4.0;

  clrscr();
  cout << "c1 = ";
  c1.print();
  cout << "\nc2 = ";
  c2.print();
  cout << "\n2 + c1 + c2 + 4 = ";
  c3.print();
  cout << "\n\n";
  getch();
  return 0;
}
```

Here is the output of the program in Listing 11.3:

```
c1 = 2 +i 3
c2 = 4 +i (-1)
2 + c1 + c2 + 4 = 12 +i 2
```

Rules for Virtual Functions

The rule for declaring a virtual function is "once virtual always virtual." In other words, after you declare a function to be virtual in a class, any subclass that overrides the virtual function must do so using another virtual function (that has the same parameter list). The virtual declaration is mandatory for the descendant classes. At first, this rule seems to lock you in. This limitation is certainly true for object-oriented programming languages that support virtual functions but not overloaded functions. In the case of C++, the workaround is interesting. You can declare nonvirtual and over-loaded functions that have the same name as the virtual function but bear a different parameter list! Moreover, you cannot inherit nonvirtual member functions that share the same name with a virtual function. Here is a simple example that illustrates the point:

```
#include <iostream.h>
class A
{
  public:
    A() {}
    virtual void foo(char c)
      { cout << "virtual A::foo() returns " << c << '\n'; }
};

class B : public A
{
  public:
    B() {}
    void foo(const char* s)
      { cout << "B::foo() returns " << s << '\n'; }
    void foo(int i)
      { cout << "B::foo() returns " << i << '\n'; }
    virtual void foo(char c)
      { cout << "virtual B::foo() returns " << c << '\n'; }
};

class C : public B
{
  public:
    C() {}
    void foo(const char* s)
      { cout << "C::foo() returns " << s << '\n'; }
    void foo(double x)
      { cout << "C::foo() returns " << x << '\n'; }
    virtual void foo(char c)
      { cout << "virtual C::foo() returns " << c << '\n'; }
};

main()
{
  int n = 100;
  A Aobj;
  B Bobj;
  C Cobj;

  Aobj.foo('A');
  Bobj.foo('B');
  Bobj.foo(10);
  Bobj.foo("Bobj");
  Cobj.foo('C');
  // if you uncomment the next statement, program does
  // not compile
  // Cobj.foo(n);
  Cobj.foo(144.123);
  Cobj.foo("Cobj");

  return 0;
}
```

This code declares three classes, A, B, and C, to form a linear hierarchy of classes. Class A declares function foo(char) as virtual. Class B also declares its own version of the virtual function foo(char). In addition, class B declares the nonvirtual overloaded functions foo(const char* s) and foo(int). Class C, the descendant of class B, declares the virtual function foo(char) and the nonvirtual and overloaded functions foo(const char*) and foo(double). Notice that class C *must* declare the foo(const char*) function if it needs the function, because it cannot inherit the member function B::foo(const char*). C++ supports a different function inheritance scheme when an overloaded and virtual function is involved. The function main() creates an instance for each of the three classes and invokes the various versions of the member function foo().

Nested Data Types

One problem plaguing C++ programmers is called *name space pollution*. This problem results from declaring too many identifiers, making the declaration of new ones likely to conflict with existing ones. C++ allows classes to reduce this problem by enabling you to declare enumerated types, structures, and even classes that are nested in classes. Although these nested types are still accessible outside their host class, you need the class name to qualify them. Consequently, this approach reduces the chances of creating new names that conflict with others.

Example of Nested Types

Consider an example. Listing 11.4 contains the source code for the LST11_04.CPP program. The program declares a class that models dynamic stacks of unsigned integers. The stack uses single-linked lists as the underlying structure.

Listing 11.4. The source code for the LST11_04.CPP program.

```
// LST11_04.CPP
// Program demonstrates data types that are nested in a class

#include <iostream.h>
#include <string.h>
```

continues

Listing 11.4. Continued

```
#include <conio.h>

class Stack
{
  protected:
    // nested structure
    struct StackNode {
        unsigned nodeData;
        StackNode *nextPtr;
    };
    // nested enumerated type
    enum boolean { false, true };
    unsigned height;   // height of stack
    StackNode *top; // pointer to the top of the stack
  public:
    Stack() : height(0), top(NULL) {}
    ~Stack() { clear(); }
    void push(unsigned);
    boolean pop(unsigned&);
    void clear();
};

void Stack::clear()
{
    unsigned x;
    while (pop(x)) /* do nothing */;
}

void Stack::push(unsigned x)
{
    StackNode *p;
    if (top) {
        p = new StackNode; // allocate new stack element
        p->nodeData = x;
     p->nextPtr = top;
     top = p;
    }
    else {
        top = new StackNode;
     top->nodeData = x;
     top->nextPtr = NULL;
    }
    height++;
}

Stack::boolean Stack::pop(unsigned& x)
{
    StackNode *p;
    if (height) {
        x = top->nodeData;
     p = top;
     top = top->nextPtr;
     delete p; // deallocate stack node
     height--;
```

```
      return true;
    }
    else
      return false;
}

main()
{
  Stack::boolean ok;
  Stack intStk;

  clrscr();
  for (unsigned x = 1; x < 7; x++) {
    cout << "Pushing " << x << " into the stack\n";
    intStk.push(x);
  }
  cout << "\nPopping off data from integer stack\n\n";
  ok = intStk.pop(x);
  while (ok) {
    cout << x << "\n";
    ok = intStk.pop(x);
  }
  cout << "\nPress any key to end the program...";
  getch();
  return 0;
}
```

The class Stack declares two nested types:

■ The StackNode structure, which contains two data members, nodeData and nextPtr. The nodeData member stores a list element (emulating a stack element). The nextPtr member is the pointer to the next list node.

■ The enumerated type boolean. I chose to declare the boolean type as a nested type rather than a global one, for the sake of demonstration. By contrast, the class implementation does not require using the StackNode structure outside the class (that is, a parameter in a member function uses that structure type).

The class Stack declares a set of data members, a constructor, a destructor, and a set of member functions. These functions support the basic stack operations, such as pushing and popping data, and clearing the stack. These member functions use the nested types to support the various operations. I would like to point out two interesting pieces of code:

■ The definition of the pop() member function uses the fully qualified name of the nested boolean type:

```
Stack::boolean Stack::pop(unsigned& x)
```

■ The function `main()` declares the boolean variable `ok`, again by using the fully qualified name of the nested boolean type:

```
Stack::boolean ok;
```

The test program performs the trivial tasks of pushing and popping data into and off the stack. Here is the output from the program in Listing 11.4:

```
Pushing 1 into the stack
Pushing 2 into the stack
Pushing 3 into the stack
Pushing 4 into the stack
Pushing 5 into the stack
Pushing 6 into the stack

Popping off data from integer stack

6
5
4
3
2
1

Press any key to end the program...
```

Friend Classes

Just as there are friend functions and friend operators, there are friend classes. C++ enables you to specify an across-the-board friendship between two classes.

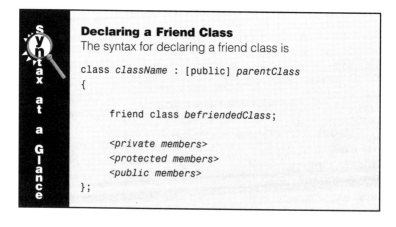

Declaring a Friend Class
The syntax for declaring a friend class is

```
class className : [public] parentClass
{

        friend class befriendedClass;

        <private members>
        <protected members>
        <public members>
};
```

The `befriendedClass` is the class that becomes a
friend to the class `className`.

Example:

In this example, the class `Matrix` is a friend of class
`Array`. This friendship is used to expand and contract
the instances of class `Array` in the functions
`Matrix::storeRow()` and `Matrix::storeCol()`.

```
class Array
{
    template class Matrix;

    protected:
        unsigned maxSize;
        double* arrPtr;
    public:
        Array(unsigned arrSize);
        ~Array();
        double& operator[](unsigned index);
        unsigned getSize() const;
};

class Matrix
{
    protected:
        unsigned maxRows;
        unsigned maxCols;
        double* matPtr;
    public:
        Matrix(unsigned numRows,
                unsigned numCols);
        ~Matrix();
        unsigned getRows() const;
        unsigned getCols() const;
        double& operator()(unsigned row,
                            unsigned col);
        boolean storeCol(Array& arr,
                            unsigned col);
        boolean recallCol(Array& arr,
                            unsigned col);
```

continues

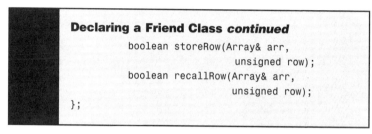

Declaring a Friend Class *continued*
```
        boolean storeRow(Array& arr,
                         unsigned row);
        boolean recallRow(Array& arr,
                          unsigned row);
    };
```

Many C++ programmers have mixed feelings about using friend classes. Conceptually, a good class design should determine a safe interface with other classes, such that there is no need for using class friendship. I have had the opportunity to code two versions of the same set of classes: one using friendship and the other without such an access privilege. My conclusion is that you should use friendship between classes only to achieve significant increase in application speed—using the access member functions of a class can add significant overhead. To bypass that overhead, use friendship between classes.

Example of Friend Classes

Consider an example that puts class friendship at work. Listing 11.5 contains the source code for the LST11_05.CPP program. The program performs simple manipulation of numerical arrays and matrices.

Listing 11.5. The source code for the LST11_05.CPP program.

```
// LST11_05.CPP
// Program demonstrates friend classes

#include <iostream.h>
#include <string.h>
#include <conio.h>

const unsigned MIN_SIZE = 3;
const unsigned MIN_ROWS = 2;
const unsigned MIN_COLS = 2;

class Array
{
    // declare that class Matrix is a friend
    friend class Matrix;

    protected:
      double *dataPtr;
      unsigned size;
```

```
    public:
      Array(unsigned Size = MIN_SIZE)
        { dataPtr = new double[size = Size]; }
      ~Array() { delete [] dataPtr; }
      unsigned getSize() const { return size; }
      double& operator [](unsigned index)
        { return *(dataPtr + index); }
};

class Matrix
{
    protected:
      double *dataPtr;
      unsigned maxRows;
      unsigned maxCols;

    public:
      Matrix(unsigned Rows = MIN_ROWS,
             unsigned Cols = MIN_COLS) :
        maxRows(Rows), maxCols(Cols)
        { dataPtr = new double[Rows * Cols]; }
      ~Matrix() { delete [] dataPtr; }
      unsigned getMaxRows() const { return maxRows; }
      unsigned getMaxCols() const { return maxCols; }
      double& operator ()(unsigned row, unsigned col)
        { return *(dataPtr + row + col * maxRows); }
      void copyRow(Array& arr, unsigned row);
};

void Matrix::copyRow(Array& arr, unsigned row)
{
  // delete array and re-create it to fit maxCols elements
  delete [] arr.dataPtr;
  arr.size = maxCols;
  arr.dataPtr = new double[arr.size];
  for (unsigned col = 0; col < maxRows; col++)
    arr[col] = *(dataPtr + row + col * maxRows);
}

main()
{
  const unsigned ARR_SIZE = 5;
  const unsigned ROWS = 3;
  const unsigned COLS = 3;

  Array ar(ARR_SIZE);
  Matrix mat(ROWS, COLS);

  clrscr();
  // assign values to array ar
  for (unsigned i = 0; i < ar.getSize(); i++)
    ar[i] = 2.5 + i * i;

  // assign values to matrix at
  for (unsigned row = 0; row < mat.getMaxRows(); row++)
```

continues

Listing 11.5. Continued

```
      for (unsigned col = 0; col < mat.getMaxCols(); col++)
        mat(row, col) = 5.5 + row + 10 * col;

    cout << "Array ar contains the following elements:\n\n";
    for (i = 0; i < ar.getSize(); i++)
      cout << "ar[" << i << "] = " << ar[i] << "\n";
    cout << "\nPress any key to continue..."; getch();

    clrscr();
    cout << "Matrix mat contains the following elements:\n\n";
    for (row = 0; row < mat.getMaxRows(); row++)
      for (col = 0; col < mat.getMaxCols(); col++)
        cout << "mat[" << row << "," << col << "] = "
             << mat(row, col) << "\n";
    cout << "\nPress any key to continue...";
    getch();

    // copy row 0 of matrix mat into array ar
    mat.copyRow(ar, 0);
    clrscr();
    cout << "Array ar contains the following elements:\n\n";
    for (i = 0; i < ar.getSize(); i++)
      cout << "ar[" << i << "] = " << ar[i] << "\n";
    cout << "\nPress any key to continue...";
    getch();
    return 0;
}
```

The program declares two classes, Array and Matrix. These classes are somewhat similar. The class Array is the same one used in Listing 11.5. I designed class Matrix to resemble class Array. I also made class Matrix a friend of class Array by placing the following declaration in class Array:

```
friend class Matrix;
```

☞ Notice that I am using the operator () (which is called the *iterator* operator in C++) to act as an extended version of the operator []. Why use the operator () to access the element of a matrix? The operator [] can accept only one parameter, which must have an integer compatible type. By contrast, the operator () can take any number and any type of parameters! Therefore, the operator () is suitable for indexing matrices and other multi-dimensional arrays.

The class Matrix has two special member functions, copyRow() and copyCol(). These functions, as their names suggest, copy matrix rows and columns into the Array-typed reference parameter arr. These functions resize the array ar to match the size of a row or column. This process is possible only by making class `Matrix` a friend of class `Array`. This relation enables the member functions of class `Matrix` to access the data members of class `Array`, `dataPtr`, and `size`, to perform the required operations.

The `main()` function performs the following tasks:

1. Declares the instance `ar` of class `Array`. The array stores five elements.

2. Declares the instance `mat` of class `Matrix`. The matrix contains three rows and three columns.

3. Assigns values to the array `ar`.

4. Assigns values to matrix `mat`.

5. Displays the elements of array `ar`.

6. Displays the elements of matrix `mat`.

7. Copies row 0 of the matrix `mat` into the array.

8. Displays the new elements of array `ar`.

Multiple Inheritance

C++ supports two types of class inheritance: single inheritance and multiple inheritance. Under single inheritance, a class has one and only one parent class. By contrast, under multiple inheritance, a class can have multiple parent classes.

Multiple inheritance is perhaps the most controversial feature of C++. Many computer scientists and programmers feel that multiple inheritance is a recipe for disaster. They regard containment (that is, declaring classes which contain data members that are themselves instances of other classes) as a much better and safer alternative to multiple inheritance.

Multiple inheritance, like containment, builds on the *HasA* notion. This notion looks at the class as containing the parent classes instead of refining them. For example, you can model an airplane by creating classes for the different components—the engine, the wings, the wheels, the fuel system, the hydraulic system, and so on. Then you create a class that models the airplane by using multiple inheritance to inherit from all the components. This scheme applies the *HasA* notion and not the *IsA* notion —an airplane is not a type of wing or an engine, or any other component. Instead, an airplane has a wing, has engines, and has the other components.

Declaring a Class Using Multiple Inheritance
The syntax for declaring a class using multiple inheritance is

```
class className : [public][virtual] parent1,
                  [public][virtual] parent2, ...
{

    private:
        <private data members>
        <private member functions>

    protected:
        <protected data members>
        <protected member functions>

    public:
        <public data members>
        <public member functions>
};
```

Example:

```
class Array
{
    protected:
        double *arrPtr;
        unsigned maxSize;
    public:
        Array(unsigned theMaxSize);
        ~Array();
        // other member functions
};

class Matrix
{
    protected:
        double *matPtr;
        unsigned maxRows;
        unsigned maxCols;
    public:
        Matrix(unsigned theMaxRows,
               unsigned theMaxCols);
        ~Matrix();
```

```
            // other member functions
    };

    class SimultEquations : public Matrix,
                            public Array
    {
        public:
            SimultEquations(unsigned theMaxRows,
                            unsigned theMaxCols);
            ~SimultEquations();
            solve();
    };
```

The keyword public works just as with single inheritance class
derivation. The keyword virtual is needed for the parent classes
that share a common ancestor class.

Example of Multiple Inheritance

Consider a short example that uses multiple inheritance. Listing
11.6 contains source code for the LST11_06.CPP program.

Listing 11.6. The source code for the LST11_06.CPP
program.

```
// LST11_06.CPP
// Program demonstrates multiple inheritance

#include <stdio.h>
#include <string.h>
#include <conio.h>

const SCREEN_CHARS = 2000;

class Cursor
{
  public:
    Cursor() {}
    void Gotoxy(int x, int y) { gotoxy(x, y); }
    void ClrScr() { clrscr(); }
    void ClrEol() { clreol(); }
    int WhereX() const { return wherex(); }
    int WhereY() const { return wherey(); }
    void pressAnyKey(const char* msg);
};
```

continues

Listing 11.6. Continued

```
class String
{
   protected:
     char s[SCREEN_CHARS];

   public:
     String() { s[0] = '\0'; }
     String(const char* str) { strcpy(s, str); }
     char* getString() { return s; }
     void setString(const char* str)
       { strcpy(s, str); }
     void prependString(const char* str);
     void appendString(const char* str) { strcat(s, str); }
     int getLen() const { return strlen(s); }
};

class Screen : public Cursor, public String
{
   public:
     Screen() { ClrScr(); }
     void prompt(const char* msg, int x, int y);
     void display(int x, int y);
};

void Cursor::pressAnyKey(const char* msg)
{
  printf("%s", msg);
  getch();
}

void String::prependString(const char* str)
{
  char ss[SCREEN_CHARS];
  strcpy(ss, str);
  strcat(ss, s);
  strcpy(s, ss);
}

void Screen::prompt(const char* msg, int x, int y)
{
  char str[SCREEN_CHARS];
  Gotoxy(x, y);
  printf("%s", msg);
  gets(str);
  setString(str);
}

void Screen::display(int x, int y)
{
```

```
  char str[SCREEN_CHARS];
  Gotoxy(x, y);
  printf("%s", getString());
}

main()
{
  Screen scrn;

  scrn.prompt("Enter your name: ", 5, 7);
  scrn.prependString("Hello ");
  scrn.appendString(". How are you?");
  scrn.display(5, 10);
  scrn.Gotoxy(5, 22);
  scrn.pressAnyKey("Press any key to end the program...");
  return 0;
}
```

Listing 11.6 declares the following classes:

1. Class Cursor models a screen cursor. The class has no data
   members and declares a default constructor as well as a set
   of member functions. The member functions perform
   common operations such as clearing the screen, clearing to
   the end of a line, getting the cursor location, and pausing
   with a message. Most of the functions are wrappers (that is,
   simple shells) for functions prototyped in the CONIO.H
   header file.

2. Class String models screen text. The class declares a single
   data member that stores up to 2,000 characters (a screenful
   of text). The class declares two constructors and a set of
   simple string-manipulating member functions.

3. Class Screen models a screen that has a cursor and text. The
   class uses multiple inheritance to inherit members from
   classes Cursor and String. The class Screen declares two
   member functions, prompt() and display(). The function
   prompt() gets a string using a prompting message that
   appears in a specified screen location. The function
   display() shows the contents of the inherited members at a
   specific screen location.

The main() function simply prompts you for your name and then
uses your input to display a greeting message.

Summary

This chapter discussed the following advanced topics related to class hierarchy design:

■ Declaring a class hierarchy enables you to derive classes from existing ones. The descendant classes inherit the members of their ancestor classes. C++ classes can override inherited member functions by defining their own versions. If you override a nonvirtual function, you can declare the new version using a different parameter list. By contrast, you cannot alter the parameter list of an inherited virtual function.

■ Virtual member functions enable your classes to support polymorphic behavior. Such behavior offers a response that is suitable for each class in a hierarchy. After you declare a function virtual, you can override it only with a virtual function in a descendant class. All versions of a virtual function in a class hierarchy must have the same signature.

■ Abstract classes empower you to specify the signature of important functions in a class hierarchy. This feature combines virtual functions and a special syntax to inform the compiler that the class contains abstract functions.

■ Overloaded member functions and operators enable a class to support more abstract expressions and statements. The various versions of an overloaded function or operator enable you to specify various combinations of valid arguments.

■ Nested data types can appear in class declarations. These types include enumerated types, structures, and even classes. Nested types represent a vehicle for limiting the problem of name space pollution. You can refer to a nested type outside its class, but you need to qualify it with the name of the host class.

■ Friend classes have the privilege of accessing all the data members of a befriended class. Such a relation enables the friend class to quickly and flexibly alter instances of the befriended classes. Such instances are typically parameters that appear in the member functions of the befriended class.

■ Multiple inheritance is a scheme that enables you to derive a class from multiple parent classes. The descendant class has access to the various members of the parent classes.

CHAPTER
TWELVE

Stream File I/O

This chapter introduces file I/O operations using the C++
stream library. Unlike the STDIO.H library in C, which has
been standardized by the ANSI C committee, the C++ stream
library has not been standardized by the C++ ANSI committee. You have a choice of using file I/O functions in the
STDIO.H file or those in the C++ stream library. Each of
these two I/O libraries offers a lot of power and flexibility. This
chapter presents basic and practical operations that enable
you to read and write data to files. In this chapter, you learn
about the following topics:

■ Common stream I/O functions

■ Sequential stream I/O for text

■ Sequential stream I/O for binary data

■ Random-access stream I/O for binary data

To learn more about the C++ stream library, consult a C++
language reference book, such as Stanley Lippman's *C++
Primer*, Second Edition, published by Addison-Wesley.

The C++ Stream Library

The C++ stream I/O library is composed of a hierarchy
of classes that are declared in several header files. The
IOSTREAM.H header file used so far is only one of these
header files. Other files include IO.H, ISTREAM.H,
OSTREAM.H, IFSTREAM.H, OFSTREAM.H, and FSTREAM.H.
The IO.H header file declares low-level classes and identifiers.
The ISTREAM.H and OSTREAM.H files support the basic input

and output stream classes. The IOSTREAM.H combines the operations of the classes in the ISTREAM.H and OSTREAM.H header files. Similarly, The IFSTREAM.H and OFSTREAM.H files support the basic file input and output stream classes. The FSTREAM.H file combines the operations of the classes in the IFSTREAM.H and OFSTREAM.H header files.

In addition to the header files mentioned, there are stream library files that offer even more specialized stream I/O. The C++ ANSI committee should define the standard stream I/O library and end any confusion regarding which classes and header files arc part of the standard stream library.

Common Stream I/O Functions

This section presents stream I/O functions that are common to both sequential and random-access I/O. These functions are detailed in the following list:

■ The `open()` function. This function enables you to open a file stream for input, output, append, and both input and output operations. This function also enables you to specify whether the related I/O is binary or text. The declaration of the `open()` function is

```
void open(const char* filename,
          int mode,
          int m = filebuf::openprot);
```

The parameter `filename` specifies the name of the file to open. The parameter `mode` indicates the I/O mode. Here is a list of arguments for parameter `mode` that are exported by the IO.H header file:

`in`	Open stream for input
`out`	Open stream for output
`ate`	Set stream pointer to the end of the file
`app`	Open stream for append mode
`trunc`	Truncate file size to 0 if it already exists
`nocreate`	Raise an error if the file does not already exist
`noreplace`	Raise an error if the file already exists
`binary`	Open in binary mode

☞ The file stream classes offer constructors that include the action (and have the same parameters) of the open() function.

■ The close() function, which closes the stream. The function takes no arguments and is declared as follows:

```
void close();
```

■ The set of basic functions that check the error status of stream operations. The following functions are included:

The good() function returns a nonzero value if there is no error in a stream operation. The declaration of the good() function is

```
int good();
```

The fail() function returns a nonzero value if there is an error in a stream operation. The declaration of the fail() function is

```
int fail();
```

The overloaded operator ! is applied to a stream instance to determine the error status.

The C++ stream libraries offer additional functions to set and query other aspects and types of stream errors.

Sequential Text Stream I/O

The functions and operators involved in sequential text I/O are simple. Moreover, you have already been exposed to most of these functions in earlier chapters. The functions and operators include

■ The stream extractor operator, <<, which writes strings and characters to a stream.

■ The stream inserter operator, >>, which reads characters from a stream.

■ The getline() function, which reads strings from a stream. The declaration of the overloaded getline() function is

```
istream& getline(signed char* buffer,
                 int size,
                 char delimiter = '\n');

istream& getline(unsigned char* buffer,
                 int size,
                 char delimiter = '\n');
```

The parameter buffer is a pointer to the string receiving the characters from the stream. The parameter size specifies the maximum number of characters to read. The parameter delimiter specifies the delimiting character that causes the string input to stop before reaching the number of characters specified by parameter size. The parameter delimiter has the default argument of '\n'.

Example of Sequential I/O

Consider a simple program that reads a text file, replaces the occurrences of a specific character in that file, and writes the output to a new file. Listing 12.1 shows the source code for the LST12_01.CPP program.

Listing 12.1. The source code for the LST12_01.CPP program.

```
// LST12_01.CPP
// Program demonstrates sequential stream file I/O

#include <fstream.h>
#include <conio.h>

enum boolean { false, true };

main()
{
  const unsigned NAME_SIZE = 64;
  const unsigned LINE_SIZE = 128;

  fstream fin, fout;
  char inFile[NAME_SIZE + 1], outFile[NAME_SIZE + 1];
  char line[LINE_SIZE + 1];
  char findChar, replChar;
  unsigned i;
  boolean ok;

  clrscr();

  do {
    ok = true;
    cout << "Enter input file: ";
    cin.getline(inFile, NAME_SIZE); cout << '\n';
    fin.open(inFile, ios::in);
    if (!fin) {
      cout << "Cannot open file " << inFile << "\n\n";
      ok = false;
    }
  } while (!ok);
```

```
do {
  ok = true;
  cout << "Enter output file: ";
  cin.getline(outFile, NAME_SIZE); cout << '\n';
  fout.open(outFile, ios::out);
  if (!fout) {
    cout << "File " << inFile << " is invalid\n\n";
    ok = false;
  }
} while (!ok);

cout << "\nEnter character to find: ";
cin >> findChar;
cout << "\nEnter character to replace: ";
cin >> replChar;
cout << "\n";

// loop to replace the characters
while (fin.getline(line, LINE_SIZE)) {
  for (i = 0; line[i] != '\0'; i++)
    if (line[i] == findChar)
      line[i] = replChar;
  // write line to the output file
  fout << line << "\n";
  // echo updated line to the screen
  cout << line << "\n";
}
// close streams
fin.close();
fout.close();
cout << "\nPress any key to end the program...";
getch();
return 0;
}
```

This program declares no classes but instead focuses on using file streams to input and output text. The main() function performs the following relevant tasks:

1. Declares the input and output file streams, fin and fout.

2. Clears the screen and prompts you to enter the input file name. The function uses a do-while loop to validate your input and to carry out the following subtasks:

   ■ Setting the flag ok to true.

   ■ Displaying the prompting message.

   ■ Getting your input using the getline() function. Here the loop uses the getline() function with the standard input stream, cin.

- Opening the input file stream, `fin`, using the function `open()`. The arguments for the function `open()` are the name of the input file and the expression `ios::in`, which specifies input mode only.

- Using the overloaded operator `!` to test whether the stream was successfully opened. If not, the loop displays an error message and assigns `false` to the variable `ok`.

3. Clears the screen and prompts you to enter the output file name. The function uses a `do-while` loop to validate your input in a manner similar to step 2. Notice that in this case, the stream function `open()` has the arguments `outFile` (the name of the output file) and `ios::out` (the expression that specifies output mode only).

4. Prompts you to enter the character to find.

5. Prompts you to enter the replacement character.

6. Uses a `while` loop to process the input lines by performing the following subtasks:

   - Reading a line from the input file stream. This subtask applies the `getline()` function to the stream `fin`.

   - Scanning the characters of the line read to locate and replace the characters that match the character in variable `findChar`.

   - Writing the updated line to the output file stream, `fout`.

   - Echoing the updated line to the standard output stream, `cout`.

7. Closes the input and output file streams.

Sequential Binary File Stream I/O

The C++ stream library offers the following stream functions for sequential binary file stream I/O:

- The function `write()` sends multiple bytes to an output stream. The overloaded function has the following declarations:

```
ostream& write(const signed char* buff, int num);
ostream& write(const unsigned char* buff, int num);
```

The parameter buff is the pointer to the buffer that contains the data to be sent to the output stream. The parameter num indicates the number of bytes in the buffer that are sent to the stream.

■ The function read() receives multiple bytes from an input stream. The overloaded function has the following declarations:

```
istream& read(signed char* buff, int num);
istream& read(unsigned char* buff, int num);
```

The parameter buff is the pointer to the buffer that receives the data from the input stream. The parameter num indicates the number of bytes to read from the stream.

Example of Sequential Binary I/O

Consider an example that performs sequential binary stream I/O. Listing 12.2 shows the source code for the LST12_02.CPP program. This program declares a class that models dynamic numerical arrays. The stream I/O operations enable the program to read and write both the individual array elements and an entire array in binary files.

Listing 12.2. The source code for the LST12_02.CPP program.

```cpp
// LST12_02.CPP
// Program demonstrates sequential binary file I/O

#include <fstream.h>
#include <conio.h>

const unsigned MIN_SIZE = 10;
const double BAD_VALUE = -1.0e+30;
enum boolean { false, true };

class Array
{
   protected:
     double *dataPtr;
     unsigned size;
     double badIndex;

   public:
     Array(unsigned Size = MIN_SIZE);
     ~Array() { delete [] dataPtr; }
```

continues

Listing 12.2. Continued

```
    unsigned getSize() const { return size; }
    double& operator [](unsigned index)
      { return (index < size) ? *(dataPtr + index)
                              : badIndex; }
    boolean writeElem(fstream& os, unsigned index);
    boolean readElem(fstream& is, unsigned index);
    boolean writeArray(const char* filename);
    boolean readArray(const char* filename);
};

Array::Array(unsigned Size)
{
  size = (Size < MIN_SIZE) ? MIN_SIZE : Size;
  badIndex = BAD_VALUE;
  dataPtr = new double[size];
}

boolean Array::writeElem(fstream& os, unsigned index)
{
    if (index < size) {
      os.write((unsigned char*)(dataPtr + index),
               sizeof(double));
      return (os.good()) ? true : false;
    }
    else
      return false;
}

boolean Array::readElem(fstream& is, unsigned index)
{
    if (index < size) {
      is.read((unsigned char*)(dataPtr + index),
              sizeof(double));
      return (is.good()) ? true : false;
    }
    else
      return false;
}

boolean Array::writeArray(const char* filename)
{
    fstream f(filename, ios::out | ios::binary);

    if (f.fail())
      return false;
    f.write((unsigned char*) &size, sizeof(size));
    f.write((unsigned char*)dataPtr, size * sizeof(double));
    f.close();
    return (f.good()) ? true : false;
}
```

```
boolean Array::readArray(const char* filename)
{
   fstream f(filename, ios::in ¦ ios::binary);
   unsigned sz;

   if (f.fail())
     return false;
   f.read((unsigned char*) &sz, sizeof(sz));
   // need to expand the array
   if (sz != size) {
     delete [] dataPtr;
     dataPtr = new double[sz];
     size = sz;
   }
   f.read((unsigned char*)dataPtr, size * sizeof(double));
   f.close();
   return (f.good()) ? true : false;
}

main()
{
  const unsigned SIZE1 = 10;
  const unsigned SIZE2 = 20;
  Array ar1(SIZE1), ar2(SIZE1), ar3(SIZE2);
  fstream f("ar1.dat", ios::out ¦ ios::binary);

  clrscr();
  // assign values to array ar1
  for (unsigned i = 0; i < ar1.getSize(); i++)
    ar1[i] = 10 * i;
  // assign values to array ar3
  for (i = 0; i < SIZE2; i++)
    ar3[i] = i;
  cout << "Array ar1 has the following values:\n";
  for (i = 0; i < ar1.getSize(); i++)
    cout << ar1[i] << "  ";
  cout << "\n\n";
  // write elements of array ar1 to the stream
  for (i = 0; i < ar1.getSize(); i++)
    ar1.writeElem(f, i);
  f.close();
  // reopen the stream for input
  f.open("ar1.dat", ios::in ¦ ios::binary);
  for (i = 0; i < ar1.getSize(); i++)
    ar2.readElem(f, i);
  f.close();
  // display the elements of array ar2
  cout << "Array ar2 has the following values:\n";
  for (i = 0; i < ar2.getSize(); i++)
    cout << ar2[i] << "  ";
  cout << "\n\n";
  // display the elements of array ar3
  cout << "Array ar3 has the following values:\n";
```

continues

Listing 12.2. Continued

```
for (i = 0; i < ar3.getSize(); i++)
  cout << ar3[i] << "   ";
cout << "\n\n";
// write the array ar3 to file AR3.DAT
ar3.writeArray("ar3.dat");
// read the array ar1 from file AR3.DAT
ar1.readArray("ar3.dat");
// display the elements of array ar1
cout << "Array ar1 now has the following values:\n";
for (i = 0; i < ar1.getSize(); i++)
  cout << ar1[i] << "   ";
cout << "\n\n\nPress any key to end the program...";
getch();
return 0;
}
```

This program declares a version of class Array that resembles versions presented in the preceding chapter. The main difference is that I added the following four member functions to perform sequential binary file stream I/O:

■ The writeElem() function writes a single array element to an output stream:

```
boolean writeElem(fstream& os, unsigned index);
```

The parameter os represents the output stream. The parameter index specifies the array element to write. The writeElem() function returns true if the argument for the index is valid and if the stream output proceeds without any error. After the writeElem() function writes an array element, the internal stream pointer advances to the next location.

■ The readElem() function reads a single array element from an input stream:

```
boolean readElem(fstream& is, unsigned index);
```

The parameter is represents the input stream. The parameter index specifies the array element to read. The readElem() function returns true if the argument for the index is valid and if the stream input proceeds without any error. After the readElem() function reads an array element, the internal stream pointer advances to the next location.

The functions writeElem() and readElem() permit the same class instance to write and read data elements from multiple streams.

■ The writeArray() function writes the entire elements of the array to a binary file:

```
boolean writeArray(const char* filename);
```

The parameter filename specifies the name of the output file. The function opens an output stream and writes the value of the data member size and then writes the elements of the dynamic array. The writeArray() function returns true if it successfully writes the array to the stream. Otherwise, the function yields false. The function opens a local output stream using the stream function open() and supplies it with the file name and I/O mode arguments. The I/O mode argument is the expression ios::out ¦ ios::binary, which specifies that the stream is opened for binary output only. The function makes two calls to the stream function write(): the first to write the data member size, and the second to write the elements of the dynamic array.

■ The readArray() function reads the entire elements of the array from a binary file:

```
boolean readArray(const char* filename);
```

The parameter filename specifies the name of the input file. The function opens an input stream and reads the value of the data member size and then reads the elements of the dynamic array. The readArray() function returns true if it successfully reads the array to the stream. Otherwise, the function yields false. The function opens a local input stream using the stream function open() and supplies it with the file name and I/O mode arguments. The I/O mode argument is the expression ios::in ¦ ios::binary, which specifies that the stream is opened for binary input only. The function makes two calls to the stream function read(): the first to read the data member size, and the second to read the elements of the dynamic array.

Another feature of function readArray() is that it resizes the instance of class Array to accommodate the data from the binary file. This means that the dynamic array accessed by the class instance can either shrink or expand, depending on the size of the array stored on file.

These four member functions indicate that the program performs two types of sequential binary stream I/O. The first type of I/O, implemented in functions readElem() and writeElem(), involves items that have the same data type. The second type of I/O, implemented in functions `readArray()` and `writeArray()`, involves items that have different data types.

The `main()` function performs the following relevant tasks:

1. Declares three instances of class `Array`: `ar1`, `ar2`, and `ar3`. The first two instances have the same dynamic array size, whereas instance `ar3` has a larger dynamic array than the other two.

2. Declares the file stream `f` and opens it (using a stream constructor) to access file AR1.DAT in binary output mode.

3. Assigns values to the instances `ar1` and `ar3`.

4. Displays the elements of instance `ar1`.

5. Writes the elements of array `ar1` to the output file stream `f`. This task uses a loop that calls the `writeElem()` function and supplies it with the arguments `f` (the file stream) and `i` (the loop control variable).

6. Closes the output file stream.

7. Opens the file stream `f` to access the data file AR1.DAT. This time, the function specifies a binary input mode.

8. Reads the elements of instance `ar2` (which has not yet been assigned any values) from the input file stream `f`. This task uses a loop that calls the `readElem()` function and supplies it with the arguments `f` (the file stream) and `i` (the loop control variable).

9. Closes the input file stream.

10. Displays the elements of instance `ar2`. These elements match those of instance `ar1`.

11. Displays the elements of instance `ar3`.

12. Writes the entire instance `ar3` using the function `writeArray()`. The argument for the `writeArray()` function call is the file name AR3.DAT.

13. Reads the array in file AR3.DAT into instance `ar1`. This task uses the `readArray()` function and supplies it the argument for the file name AR3.DAT.

14. Displays the new elements of instance `ar1`.

Here is the output from a session with the program in Listing 12.2:

```
Array ar1 has the following values:
0  10  20  30  40  50  60  70  80  90

Array ar2 has the following values:
0  10  20  30  40  50  60  70  80  90

Array ar3 has the following values:
0  1  2  3  4  5  6  7  8  9  10  11  12  13  14  15  16  17  18  19

Array ar1 now has the following values:
0  1  2  3  4  5  6  7  8  9  10  11  12  13  14  15  16  17  18  19


Press any key to end the program...
```

Random-Access File Stream I/O

Random-access file stream operations also use the stream functions
read() and write(), presented in a previous section. The stream
library offers a set of stream seeking functions to enable you to
move the stream pointer to any valid location. The function seekg()
is one such function. This overloaded function has the following
declaration:

```
istream& seekg(long pos);
istream& seekg(long pos, seek_dir dir);
```

The parameter pos in the first version specifies the absolute byte
position in the stream. In the second version, the parameter pos
specifies a relative offset based on the argument for parameter dir.
The arguments for the latter parameter are shown in the following
table:

ios::beg	From the beginning of the file
ios::cur	From the current position of the file
ios::end	From the end of the file

Example of Random-Access I/O

Consider an example that uses random-access file stream I/O. The
next program implements a virtual (that is, disk-based) array. Accessing the different array elements requires random-access I/O.
Listing 12.3 shows the source code for the LST12_03.CPP program.

Listing 12.3. The source code for the LST12_03.CPP program.

```
// LST12_03.CPP
// Program demonstrates random-access binary file I/O

#include <fstream.h>
#include <conio.h>
#include <stdlib.h>

const unsigned MIN_SIZE = 5;
const double BAD_VALUE = -1.0e+30;
enum boolean { false, true };

class VmArray
{
   protected:
     fstream f;
     unsigned size;
     double badIndex;

   public:
     VmArray(unsigned Size, const char* filename);
     ~VmArray() { f.close(); }
     unsigned getSize() const { return size; }
     boolean writeElem(double x, unsigned index);
     boolean readElem(double& x, unsigned index);
     void Combsort();
};

VmArray::VmArray(unsigned Size, const char* filename)
{
  size = (Size < MIN_SIZE) ? MIN_SIZE : Size;
  badIndex = BAD_VALUE;
  f.open(filename, ios::in | ios::out | ios::binary);
  if (f.good()) {
    // fill the file stream with zeros
    double x = 0.0;
    f.seekg(0);
    for (unsigned i = 0; i < size; i++)
      f.write((unsigned char*) &x, sizeof(double));
  }
}

boolean VmArray::writeElem(double x, unsigned index)
{
   if (index < size) {
     f.seekg(index * sizeof(double));
     f.write((unsigned char*)&x, sizeof(double));
     return (f.good()) ? true : false;
   }
```

```
    else
      return false;
}

boolean VmArray::readElem(double &x, unsigned index)
{
   if (index < size) {
     f.seekg(index * sizeof(double));
     f.read((unsigned char*)&x, sizeof(double));
     return (f.good()) ? true : false;
   }
   else
     return false;
}

void VmArray::Combsort()
{
   unsigned i, j, gap = size;
   boolean inOrder;
   double xi, xj;

   do {
     gap = gap * 8 / 11;
     gap = (gap < 1) ? 1 : gap;
     inOrder = true;
     for (i = 0, j = gap; i < (size - gap); i++, j++) {
       readElem(xi, i);
       readElem(xj, j);
       if (xi > xj) {
         inOrder = false;
         writeElem(xi, j);
         writeElem(xj, i);
       }
     }
   } while (!(inOrder && gap == 1));
}

main()
{
  VmArray ar(10, "ar.dat");
  double x;

  clrscr();
  // assign random values to array ar
  for (unsigned i = 0; i < ar.getSize(); i++) {
    x = (double) (1 + random(1000));
    ar.writeElem(x, i);
  }
  cout << "Unsorted array is\n";
  for (i = 0; i < ar.getSize(); i++) {
```

continues

Listing 12.3. Continued

```
    ar.readElem(x, i);
    cout << x << ' ';
}
ar.Combsort(); // sort array
cout << "\n\nSorted array is\n";
for (i = 0; i < ar.getSize(); i++) {
  ar.readElem(x, i);
  cout << x << ' ';
}
cout << "\n\nPress any key to end the program...";
getch();
return 0;
}
```

The class VmArray models a disk-based dynamic array that stores all of its elements in a random-access binary file. Notice that the class declares an instance of class fstream and that there is no pointer to a dynamic array. The class declares a constructor, a destructor, and a set of member functions.

The class constructor has two parameters: Size and filename. The parameter Size specifies the size of the virtual array. The parameter filename names the binary file that stores the elements of a class instance. The constructor opens the stream f using the stream function open() and supplies the argument of parameter filename and the I/O mode expression ios::in ¦ ios::out ¦ ios::binary. This expression specifies that the stream is opened for binary input and output mode (that is, random-access mode). If the constructor successfully opens the file stream, it fills the file with zeros. The class destructor performs the simple task of closing the file stream f.

The functions writeElem() and readElem() support the random access of array elements. These functions use the stream function seekg() to position the stream pointer at the appropriate array element. The writeElem() function then calls the stream function write() to store an array element (supplied by the parameter x). By contrast, the function readElem() calls the stream function read() to retrieve an array element (returned by the parameter x). Both functions return boolean results that indicate the success of the I/O operation.

The VmArray class also declares the Combsort() function to sort the elements of the virtual array. This function uses the readElem() and writeElem() member functions to access and swap the array elements.

The main() function performs the following relevant tasks:

1. Declares the instance ar, of class VmArray. This instance stores 10 elements in the binary file AR.DAT.

2. Assigns random values to the elements of instance ar. This task uses a loop that creates random numbers and assigns them to the local variable x. Then the loop writes the value in x to the instance ar by calling the function writeElem(). The arguments for the call to writeElem() are x and i (the loop control variable).

3. Displays the unsorted elements of instance ar.

4. Sorts the array by invoking the Combsort() member function.

5. Displays the sorted elements of instance ar.

Here is the output from a sample session with the program in Listing 12.3:

```
Unsorted array is
11 4 336 34 356 218 537 196 701 950

Sorted array is
4 11 34 196 218 336 356 537 701 950

Press any key to end the program...
```

Summary

This chapter gave you a brief introduction to the C++ stream I/O library. The chapter discussed the following topics:

■ Common stream I/O functions. These stream functions include open(), close(), good(), fail(), and the operator !. The function open(), as the name suggests, opens a file for stream I/O and supports alternate and multiple I/O modes. The function close() shuts down a file stream. The functions good() and fail() indicate the success or failure of a stream I/O operation.

■ Sequential stream I/O for text. C++ enables you to perform this kind of stream I/O using the operators << and >>, as well as the stream function getline(). The operator << can write characters and strings (as well as the other predefined data types). The operator >> is suitable for getting characters. The function getline() enables your applications to read strings from the keyboard or from a text file.

- Sequential stream I/O for binary data, which uses the stream functions `write()` and `read()` to write and read data from any kind of variables.

- Random-access stream I/O for binary data, which uses the `seekg()` function with the functions `read()` and `write()`. The `seekg()` function enables you to move the stream pointer to either absolute or relative byte locations in the stream.

INDEX

Symbols

! (logical NOT) operator, 36
!= (not equal to) operator, 36
menu (IDE), 7
#define directive, 19-20
#error directive, 21
#if directive, 22
#ifdef directive, 23
#ifndef directive, 23
#include directive, 20-21
#line directive, 23-24
#pragma directive, 24-26
#undef directive, 20
% (modulus) arithmetic operator, 32
%= arithmetic assignment operator, 34
& (bitwise AND) operator, 38
&& (logical AND) operator, 36
&= bit manipulation assignment operator, 38
* (multiply) arithmetic operator, 32
*= arithmetic assignment operator, 34
+ (add) arithmetic operator, 31
+ (unary plus) arithmetic operator, 31

++ increment operators, 32-33
+= arithmetic assignment operator, 34
- (subtract) arithmetic operator, 32
- (unary minus) arithmetic operator, 31
-- decrement operators, 32-33
-= arithmetic assignment operator, 34
/ (divide) arithmetic operator, 32
/= arithmetic assignment operator, 34
< (less than) operator, 36
<< (bitwise shift left) operator, 38
<< (stream extractor) operator, 193
<<= bit-manipulation assignment operator, 38
<= (less than or equal to) operator, 36
≡ menu (System menu), 13
== (equal to) operator, 36
> (greater than) operator, 36

Disk Offer

The programs in this book are available on disk from the author. The cost of the disk is $6 in the U.S. and Canada, and $10 for overseas orders. Please make your check payable to **Namir Shammas**. When ordering outside the U.S., send a check drawn on a U.S. bank to the following address. Sorry, no purchase orders or credit cards.

> Namir Shammas
> 3928 Margate Dr.
> Richmond, VA 23235

Name _____

Company (for company address) _____

Address _____

City _____

State or province _____

ZIP or postal code _____

Please specify disk size:

    5¼ inch ____

    3½ inch ____

This offer is made by Namir Shammas, not by Que Corporation.